WELCOME

IWM Duxford is a museum like no other.

It was from RAF Duxford that airmen from Britain, Belgium, Czechoslovakia, Poland and throughout the Commonwealth took to the skies to fight for freedom in the Battle of Britain. And it was from this same airfield later in the war that American Thunderbolts and Mustangs took off to carry the fight deep into Hitler's Germany.

This illustrious past is present all around you — it's the same airfield, the same buildings, the same sights, sounds and smells. Spitfires still roar overhead, footsteps echo across hangar floors, fumes linger in the air. It's the kind of history that you can live and breathe.

But IWM Duxford is about more than the Second World War. It's about over a century of military aviation in Britain, the Commonwealth and America. And it's also about size, scale and space. Inside every hangar and exhibition hall — and outside them too — there are hundreds of large aircraft, vehicles, boats and weapons that other museums would struggle to house. You can walk around them, inside them, above them and below them. You can see them being restored and conserved. You can discover stories about the people whose lives they have affected. And, above all, you can enjoy the time and space to think about what it all means.

We hope you enjoy the experience.

1	AirSpace
2	Flying Aircraft
HD	Historic Duxford
3	Air and Sea
4	Battle of Britain
5	Conservation in Action
6	1940 Operations Room
7	American Air Museum
8	Land Warfare
↘	Exhibition entrances

8

7 The American
Air Museum Café

OPEN
Mar-Oct

5

6

4

The Workshop
Restaurant

3

HD

2

Where to find...

Airborne Assault

Airfield

Café and restaurant

Classic Wings
Pleasure Flights

Clore Learning Centre

Concorde
(restricted opening times)

Duxford Radio Society

First Aid

Playground

Prefab Bungalow

Royal Anglian
Regiment Museum
and Memorial

Shop

Tank Arena

Toilets

The Armoury Café
and Kitchen

P

Visitor Centre
Museum entrance / exit

1

CONTENTS

ESSENTIAL IWM DUXFORD 4

INTRODUCING IWM DUXFORD 6

THE STORY OF HISTORIC DUXFORD 12
Discover the role that Duxford played in
both the First and Second World Wars, and
how it became the museum that it is today

AIR SHOWS AND EVENTS 20

AIRSPACE 22
Follow the story of aviation in Britain and the
Commonwealth, and find out more about
the aircraft on display in the extraordinary
AirSpace hangar

AIR AND SEA 30

BATTLE OF BRITAIN 32
Find out how Duxford played its part in the
momentous air battle that helped to shape
the course of the Second World War

1940 OPERATIONS ROOM 40

AMERICAN AIR MUSEUM 42
Explore the key role played by American air
power in 20th- and 21st-century conflict,
and the vital part that Britain played in the story

CONSERVATION IN ACTION 50

LAND WARFARE 52
Discover how the experience of war on
the battlefield has changed for British and
Commonwealth troops since the days of
the First World War

PARTNER MUSEUMS 60

IWM DUXFORD AND YOU 62

ABOUT IWM 64

REAL LIFE STORIES

As you look through your guidebook, watch out for
the regular **In Their Own Words** sections, where
you'll find stories about Duxford, its history and its
exhibits.

Some are told by veterans who flew from Duxford
during the war. Some relate to particular aircraft,
boats or vehicles that you can see in the hangars.
Others are the thoughts of people connected
to the museum today – from display pilots to
conservationists. All of them reveal something to
helps bring your experience of IWM Duxford to life.

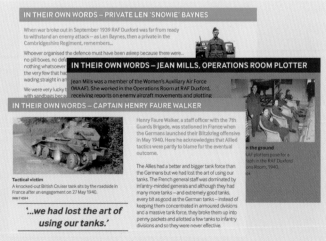

IN THEIR OWN WORDS – PRIVATE LEN 'SNOWIE' BAYNES

When war broke out in September 1939 RAF Duxford was far from ready
to withstand an enemy attack – as Len Baynes, then a private in the
Cambridgeshire Regiment, remembers.

Whoever organised the defence must have been asleep because there were
no pill boxes, no defe...
nothing whatsoever...
the very few that ha...
wading straight in an...

We were very lucky t...
with sandbags becau...

IN THEIR OWN WORDS – CAPTAIN HENRY FAURE WALKER

IN THEIR OWN WORDS – JEAN MILLS, OPERATIONS ROOM PLOTTER

Jean Mills was a member of the Women's Auxiliary Air Force
(WAAF). She worked in the Operations Room at RAF Duxford,
receiving reports on enemy aircraft movements and plotting

Tactical victim
A knocked-out British Cruiser tank sits by the roadside in
France after an engagement on 27 May 1940.
IWM F 4594

'...we had lost the art of
using our tanks.'

Henry Faure Walker, a staff officer with the 7th
Guards Brigade, was stationed in France when
the Germans launched their Blitzkrieg offensive
in May 1940. Here he acknowledges that Allied
tactics were partly to blame for the eventual
outcome.

The Allies had a better and bigger tank force than
the Germans but we had lost the art of using our
tanks. The French general staff was dominated by
infantry-minded generals and although they had
many more tanks – and extremely good tanks,
every bit as good as the German tanks – instead of
keeping them concentrated in armoured divisions
and a massive tank force, they broke them up into
penny packets and allotted a few tanks to infantry
divisions and so they were never effective.

ESSENTIAL IWM DUXFORD

There are countless experiences to be enjoyed at IWM Duxford — not least the chance, in fine weather, to see historic aircraft flying overhead. In every hangar and exhibition hall there are aircraft, vehicles, objects, stories and reconstructions that you simply must not miss.

GET INTERACTIVE

The upper floor of **AirSpace** is a great place to start your visit. Have fun pressing buttons, pulling levers, turning wheels and touching screens to discover how aircraft fly, how they are made and how they have developed over the years.

IWM_SITE_DUX_001666

BOARD CONCORDE

Head to the lower floor of **AirSpace** to pick your favourite from the aircraft that surround you. Climb on board **Concorde**, marvel at the extraordinary engineering of the **Sunderland flying boat,** and get up close to the **de Havilland DH9** — a bomber which flew out of IWM Duxford during the First World War.

IWM_SITE_DUX_000575

PAY TRIBUTE TO THE FEW

Discover the story of IWM Duxford's finest hour in the **Battle of Britain** exhibition. See for yourself the aircraft that fought each other so fiercely in the fateful summer of 1940 – the **Messerschmitt Bf109**, the **Hawker Hurricane** shown here (it's an Mk IIB painted to represent an Mk IIA of No. 111 Squadron in 1940) and, of course, the iconic **Supermarine Spitfire**.

IWM_SITE_DUX_000458

MEET THE BEST

Look out for record-breaking aircraft like the beautifully sleek **Lockheed SR-71A Blackbird** in the **American Air Museum** (left, and on p.48). It's the fastest air-breathing jet aircraft ever built, and the highest flying. The dark blue paint acted as camouflage against the night sky and increased the emission of internal heat.

IWM_SITE_DUX_001586

AND DON'T MISS

GO BACK IN TIME

See IWM Duxford as it was in wartime. Visit the reconstructed **Watch Office**, relive a German raid on the airfield in the **1940 Operations Room**, and explore the **Historic Duxford** exhibition where you'll meet the many men and women who served their countries here. IWM 2013_010_027

The section of fabric from the **Wright Flyer** – the ingenious aircraft that launched the age of aviation – on display in **AirSpace**.

IWM_SITE_DUX_001667

The caravans in **Land Warfare** from which Montgomery ran his Second World War campaigns – from El Alamein to Normandy.

IWM_2009_059_007

The chance to watch up close as conservators work on historic aircraft – in **Flying Aircraft** and **Conservation in Action**.

IWM_SITE_DUX_001645

INTRODUCING IWM DUXFORD

IWM Duxford is renowned as one of the world's leading aviation museums, housing an extraordinary collection of historic aircraft. But it is also much more than that.

IWM Duxford stands apart from other aviation museums because its site is an exhibit in itself. The airfield has a history that stretches back to the First World War — with most of the original hangars still standing to prove it.

It also played a central role in some of the most dramatic days in 20th-century history — serving as a base for many of the Spitfire and Hurricane pilots who fought the Luftwaffe in the Battle of Britain.

Discover the stories of IWM Duxford in exhibitions such as **Historic Duxford, Battle of Britain** and the **1940 Operations Room**. You can also read more about them in this guidebook:

The Story of Historic Duxford   p.12

Battle of Britain   p.32

1940 Operations Room   p.40

'From May to October 1940 we were all stretched to the limits of our endurance.'

Woody Woodhall, RAF Duxford Station Commander

7

Room to explore (left)
This aerial view of IWM Duxford shows just how large the site is, with exhibition spaces and civil aircraft ranged alongside the air field.
IWM_SITE_DUX_000170

8 **Quick and deadly**
The de Havilland Mosquito was the most
effective and fastest bomber of the Second
World War. It relied on speed for its defence.
The aircraft on display in AirSpace was built
as a bomber and then later converted to a
target-tub, which is how it is configured today.
IWM_SITE_DUX_001575

AVIATION SHOWCASE

People come to IWM Duxford from all over the world
to see its remarkable collection of aircraft. Spread
out across several exhibition spaces, the collection
spans the entire history of military aviation, offering
a tangible record of how air power has come to
dominate the way in which wars are fought.

One of the most breathtaking displays can be found
in the massive purpose-built **AirSpace**, telling the
story of aviation in Britain and the Commonwealth.
Equally impressive is the **American Air Museum**,
looking at the collaboration between Britain and
America, and how American air power has played a
key part in conflict in the 20th and 21st centuries.

You can find out more about these exhibitions and
the stories that they tell in this guidebook:

AirSpace   **p.22**

American Air Museum   **p.42**

WORKING AIRFIELD

IWM Duxford is a place where propellers still turn and chocks are still pulled away. You can stand within a few yards of vintage aircraft as they prepare to take off, and then watch them swoop and soar in the skies above your head.

It's also a place where engine oil is still changed and filters are still cleaned. You can see engineers readying their historic 'war birds' for flight in **Flying Aircraft**, and you can watch what it takes to preserve aircraft for future generations in **Conservation in Action**.

Flying Aircraft	p.21
Conservation in Action	p.50

Thrillingly close (upper left)
The air pulsates as the IWM's Supermarine Spitfire IA, N3200, takes off. IWM 2015_046_069

Work you can watch (lower left)
IWM Duxford's F-15 in the Conservation in Action hangar. IWM 2015_013_007

MORE THAN AIRCRAFT

IWM Duxford's size makes it the perfect place to exhibit all sorts of large objects that would otherwise need to be stored away from public eyes. This means that you can find far more than just aircraft on the site.

Some – like the boats and submarines on display in **Air and Sea**, and the tanks, weapons and vehicles exhibited in **Land Warfare** – are grouped together in specific exhibition spaces. Others – like the section of a V1 flying bomb ramp – are displayed outside as you walk from hangar to hangar.

Air and Sea	p.30
Land Warfare	p.52

Staring down the barrel (above)
The US 155mm M40 Self-Propelled Gun is displayed in Land Warfare. Introduced at the end of the Second World War, it went on to see major action in Korea.
IWM_SITE_DUX_001566

BEYOND BRITAIN

You can find well over one hundred aircraft at IWM Duxford, and scores more vehicles, boats and artillery pieces.

Many are British in origin, but many hail from beyond these shores – from the Commonwealth, as well as from America, Russia, France, Argentina, Italy and Germany.

All of them have their own stories to tell about the impact of war across the globe.

World leaders (above)
The General Dynamics F-111E – the world's first 'swing wing' combat aircraft – is reinstalled during the redevelopment of the American Air Museum. Above it is the Douglas C-47 Skytrain, the most widely used military aircraft of the Second World War.
© JOHN HUGHES

INDIVIDUAL STORIES

There are stories behind every object on display at IWM Duxford – every aircraft, tank and gun, every medal, photograph and flying jacket. Some are about the people who owned them or used them. Others are about the men, women and children whose lives were affected by them. All of them reveal something about what war is really like.

Some of these stories are all the more powerful because they are about events that took place at Duxford itself – set in the same historic structures and under these same skies. Telling these stories is a large part of what IWM Duxford is about.

Cast of characters

Top row (from left): Sergeant Bohumir Furst of 310 Squadron (1940); a group of servicemen in the Operations Block at Duxford (c.1940).

Middle row (from left): Members of the WRAF in the Motor Transport yard at Duxford, 1918; Squadron Leader Douglas Bader at RAF Duxford, 1940; Servicemen (and dog) at Duxford airfield, 1919.

Bottom row (from left): A group of servicemen and servicewomen at Duxford, 1950s; US airmen of the 78th Fighter Group, c.1944.

IWM CH 1296; IWM HU 46197; IWM HU 40586; IWM CH 1341; IWM HU 40572; IWM HU 50654; IWM HU 33306

THE STORY OF HISTORIC DUXFORD

Duxford is most famous for the role that it played during the Battle of Britain in the Second World War, but its history stretches back to the previous war, when aircraft were first used to gain an advantage over enemy forces.

The First World War saw the sky become part of the battlefield for the first time. Armies locked in trench warfare relied on intelligence from reconnaissance aircraft to formulate their plans and aim their guns. Bombs dropped from German airships brought the shock of war to the homes of ordinary British citizens. And the addition of machine guns turned aircraft on both sides into a new breed of fighter.

The need for pilots – and airfields – became ever more urgent, and teams from the War Office were despatched to identify suitable locations. In 1916 one was found in an area of farmland north-west of the small village of Duxford, and work began in 1917 to turn it into an airfield where new pilots could be trained.

By the end of the war, in November 1918, No. 35 Training Depot Station was a place of work for some 850 men and women, including members of the US Air Service, who helped to maintain the aircraft. Most crucially of all, a total of 126 new pilots had graduated from Duxford to serve with the newly formed Royal Air Force.

DID YOU KNOW?

In the First World War even training to be a pilot was a dangerous business. Duxford produced 126 airmen in the final months of the war, but it lost 13 men to fatal training accidents in the same period.

13

Duxford is born (left)

An aerial view of the Duxford site during its development in 1918. Many of the technical buildings remain today, including three of the 'Belfast Truss' hangars. The largest buildings visible in this photograph, they are so-named because this type of roof structure was first used in Belfast in the nineteenth century.

IWM Q 96065

1924–1939:
BUILDING FOR WAR

After the First World War Duxford was placed on a list of military sites to be cared for and maintained while a decision was made about their future. It then reopened again in 1920 as No. 2 Flying Training School.

Over the following years the airfield forged strong links with Cambridge University, most notably in a research collaboration with its engineering department. One of the students involved was Frank Whittle, who went on to invent the jet engine. Then, in 1925, Duxford became home to the Cambridge University Air Squadron.

Throughout the early 1920s the British government was giving thought to how a future war might be fought. It was clear that aerial warfare would play a crucial role; it was predicted, for example, that London would be bombarded by up to 200 tons of bombs in the first 24 hours of any new conflict.

In 1923 it was decided to reorganise Britain's air defences to combat this threat. The following year,

as part of this plan, Duxford became an operational fighter station – a role it would go on to serve with distinction for 37 years.

In 1933 Adolf Hitler, head of the Nazi Party, came to power in Germany and quickly began putting an aggressive foreign policy into action. Tensions across Europe started to rise, and RAF Duxford really began to grow in size and importance. In 1936, for example, 19 Squadron at Duxford was split and expanded to become 19 and 66 squadrons. Then, in 1938, as Europe was rocked by the Munich Crisis, they became the first RAF squadrons to have their Gloster Gauntlets replaced with Supermarine Spitfires. This was a daunting but exhilarating prospect for Duxford's pilots – the Spitfire was 216km/hr (134mph) faster than the Gauntlet and had eight rather than two guns.

As it turned out, this expansion and rearmament barely came fast enough for RAF Duxford, as renewed tension in the summer of 1939 ended with Britain going to war.

DID YOU KNOW?

A flight of captured German aircraft flew from Duxford during the Second World War where they were evaluated and then demonstrated to other Allied units. Perhaps inevitably, the unit was nicknamed the 'Rafwaffe'.

Learning to fly (left)
Five trainee pilots pose in their helmets, goggles and flying suits at No 2 Flying Training School, Duxford, 1921.
IWM HU 41572

IWM DUXFORD TIMELINE

Duxford has a story that stretches back a hundred years. It was here that pilots learned to fly the revolutionary bi-planes of the First World War, here that the RAF's first Spitfires took to the skies, and here that a discarded Cold War airfield was transformed into an award-winning museum. Here are the key moments in that story.

1917–1918

An area of farmland near Duxford is developed to become No. 35 Training Depot Station. By the end of the First World War it has provided 126 new pilots.

1919

Flying from Duxford is called to a halt after the First World War, but starts again in 1920 with the opening of the No. 2 Flying Training School.

IN THEIR OWN WORDS – PRIVATE LEN 'SNOWIE' BAYNES

When war broke out in September 1939 RAF Duxford was far from ready to withstand an enemy attack – as Len Baynes, then a private in the Cambridgeshire Regiment, remembers...

Whoever organised the defence must have been asleep because there were... no pill boxes, no defensive positions, no trenches round the camp... There was nothing whatsoever to stop Duxford – that absolute key aerodrome... one of the very few that had Spitfires – nothing whatsoever to stop the Germans just wading straight in and obliterating it.

We were very lucky that they didn't attack. We started work... building pillboxes with sandbags because we hadn't got any facilities for making concrete pillboxes... And we built... a machine gun post on the top of one of the hangars, with a series of ladders to get us up there. [But] we had no automatic weapons because the battalion only had one and they needed that to train the rest of the men!'

Private Len 'Snowie' Baynes
Baynes went on to fight in Singapore and was captured by the Japanese.
© LEN BAYNES

1939 – 1943: THE FINEST HOUR

Late in the morning on 3 September 1939 the communications office at RAF Duxford received signal A34. It confirmed what Prime Minister Neville Chamberlain had already announced on radio: Britain was at war with Germany.

Work to prepare the base for conflict was still ongoing, with camouflage paint still to be applied in some places and accommodation to be organised for the expected influx of Women's Auxiliary Air Force (WAAF) personnel.

Likewise the RAF had still to settle on the best way to use its resources – including Duxford, which was now a sector station of No. 12 Group Fighter Command. Eventually a 'Big Wing' of five squadrons, including No. 310 Squadron based at RAF Duxford, flew from Duxford and Fowlmere (Duxford's satellite airfield) – led by Squadron Leader Douglas Bader.

The base therefore played an important role in the summer of 1940 when the Germans, buoyed by dramatic success on the European mainland, launched a campaign to take control of the skies above southern England. Turn to pages 32–39 for the story of this 'Battle of Britain', in which the RAF managed to defeat the German Luftwaffe and so force Hitler to shelve his plans for an invasion.

For the next two and a half years Duxford also played host to various specialist units, tasked with developing and evaluating potentially vital new equipment – from calibrating radar stations to devising better gun mountings. It was also the base for the RAF's first Hawker Typhoon wing, which flew in support of a raid on Dieppe in August 1942.

1924
Duxford becomes an operational fighter station. It expands in the 1930s to meet the growing threat of Adolf Hitler's Nazi Germany.

1938
Duxford's 19 and 66 Squadrons become the first to start replacing their Gloster Gauntlets with Supermarine Spitfires.

SEPTEMBER 1939
The Second World War begins. By June 1940 the British Army is being evacuated from France (left), and Germany looks poised to invade.
IWM H 1623

1943 – 1945:
THE AMERICAN YEARS

On 7 December 1941 Japan attacked the US naval base at Pearl Harbor, so bringing America into the war. Throughout 1942 scores of new airfields were built in eastern and southern England to accommodate the incoming might of the United States Army Air Force (USAAF), and the RAF also handed over some of its own bases.

By April 1943 it was the turn of RAF Duxford, which became Station 357 of the US 8th Air Force – home to the 82nd, 83rd and 84th Fighter Squadrons of the 78th Fighter Group. The full-throated roar of the Spitfire was replaced with the rumble of the P-47 Thunderbolt and, from December 1944, the high-pitched whistle of the P-51 Mustang.

These fighters accompanied American bombers on daylight raids over occupied Europe and Germany, engaging enemy fighters and attacking ground targets. During 1943 and 1944 they helped to destroy much of Germany's fighter strength – a key part of the preparations for an Allied invasion of north-west Europe.

When dawn came on the day of the invasion – 6 June 1944 – P-47 Thunderbolts from Duxford support the invaders by attacking targets further inland. Then, as the Allies pressed inland, the 78th Fighter Group earned two Distinguished Unit Citations – the first for a flak suppression mission in September 1944, the second for the destruction of 135 enemy aircraft on airfields in eastern Germany in April 1945.

But such success came at a cost. By the time the war came to an end in August 1945, a total of 113 US pilots had lost their lives flying from Duxford.

IN THEIR OWN WORDS – LT COL HAYDEN RICHARDS, P-47 PILOT

The 78th Fighter Group enjoyed great success attacking enemy aircraft on the ground. Here US pilot Lieutenant Colonel Hayden Richards remembers just how dangerous such attacks were...

Strafing was the most difficult mission of all. There was always someone out there to kill you, you know.

What you would attempt to do is employ the element of surprise. In other words you didn't circle above and then go down. You saw [an] airfield when you were escorting the bombers, so after you left the bombers and you were coming back you had that airfield in mind.

And you were tempted, as an element of surprise, to come in and make one pass. You had to line up and get an aircraft in your sight, fire and then take off. It was suggested that you don't tempt fate – that is come back for the second run or the third run. Unfortunately many [of our other pilots] did that and it cost them.

Bolt from the blue
Airmen of the 78th Fighter Group pose in front of a P-47 Thunderbolt.
IWM FRE 2993

10 JULY 1940
The Battle of Britain begins as the Luftwaffe vies with the RAF for control of the skies over southern England. For Duxford's role, see pages 32–39.

7 DECEMBER 1941
Japan attacks the US naval base at Pearl Harbor (right), bringing the might of America's ground, naval and air forces into the war.
IWM NYF 22545

1942
The first Hawker Typhoon Wing is formed at Duxford, and flies in support of the ill-fated Dieppe raid in August 1942.

Ready to fly (above)
American airmen leave the 78th
Fighter Group's Briefing Room in
Hangar 4 at Duxford to walk towards
the airfield. Today Hangar 4 houses
the Battle of Britain exhibition.
IWM HU 31927

DID YOU KNOW?
The steam-heated brick buildings
at Duxford made for a much more
comfortable war than the hastily
constructed tin huts at other
airfields. American airmen were
so impressed that they dubbed
the base 'the Country Club of the
European Theatre of Operations'.

APRIL 1943
Duxford is taken over by
the US 8th Air Force. It
plays host to the P-47
Thunderbolts and P-51
Mustangs of the 78th
Fighter Group.

1943–1944
The 78th Fighter Group flies
in support of dangerous
daylight bombing raids
over occupied Europe and
Germany.

6 JUNE 1944
The Allies land an invasion
force in France, with P-47
Thunderbolts from Duxford
flying in support of the
Allied fleet invasion.

SEPTEMBER 1944
The 78th Fighter Group
undertakes dangerous
flak suppression missions
over Germany, earning itself
a Distinguished Unit Citation.

APRIL 1945
The 78th Fighter Group flies six-hour missions over eastern Germany, earning a second Distinguished Unit Citation for a particularly successful raid on 16 April.

DECEMBER 1945
Four months after the war in Europe comes to an end, the USAAF hands Duxford back to the RAF.

1950s
Duxford evolves to meet the Cold War threat of Soviet bombers. By 1958 it is home to subsonic jet fighters: the Gloster Javelin and the Hawker Hunter.

JULY 1961
Deemed unsuitable to be a base for supersonic jet fighters, Duxford is taken out of service.

1946 – 1961: THE COLD WAR

In December 1945 the United States Army Air Forces handed Duxford back to the RAF. The war had been over for only four months, but cracks were already appearing in relations between the western powers and their eastern front ally the Soviet Union.

Differences in political ideology fuelled an atmosphere of mutual suspicion, which escalated into a tense military stand-off. It was the start of a new Cold War that would last for over 40 years.

Britain's post-war priority was therefore to defend itself against the threat of Soviet bombers – and Duxford was at the forefront of the effort. In October 1946 the airfield welcomed its first jet fighter – the Gloster Meteor – and in the 1950s there came the sub-sonic Gloster Javelin and Hawker Hunter.

However, the development of Britain's first supersonic jet fighter, the English Electric Lightning, spelled the end for the airbase. It entered service in 1960 and required a better runway than Duxford could offer.

The end came swiftly. On 31 July 1961 a Gloster Meteor NF 14 sped its way into the East Anglian skies – the last official RAF flight to take off from the base. Less than a year later, weeds and grass had begun to take hold on the concrete apron and runway. Duxford was falling into disrepair.

Ushering in the jet age (left)
RAF Duxford's 66 Squadron shows off some of its Gloster Meteor jet fighters in July 1949. You can see a Gloster Meteor up close in the Battle of Britain exhibition hangar.
IWM MH 28313

DID YOU KNOW?
In 1968 one of Duxford's hangars was deliberately blown up during the making of the film *The Battle of Britain*. The explosion looked great on camera, but it is not clear if the Ministry of Defence had given its permission!

1962 – PRESENT: A NEW PURPOSE

For most of the 1960s Duxford faced an uncertain future. Eventually, in 1968, the Ministry of Defence invited proposals for how the site could be used. One bidder suggested turning it into a recreation centre, another a prison. But the Imperial War Museum (IWM) and the East Anglian Aviation Society proposed the idea of a museum.

The process dragged on for several years, but in the meantime IWM was given permission to store aircraft on the site, and in October 1973 it helped put on the site's first air show since its RAF days.

Finally, in 1975, came the decision to transfer the site permanently into the care of IWM and the newly formed Duxford Aviation Society. The following summer the gates of the airfield were opened up to the public on a daily basis, and tens of thousands flocked to see the many aircraft and large objects that the museum had chosen to store there.

Tens of thousands became hundreds of thousands, and hundreds of thousands became millions. Huge new exhibition spaces were added, including **Land Warfare** in 1992, the **American Air Museum** in 1997 and **AirSpace** in 2007. As it enters its second century of existence, Duxford continues to go from strength to strength.

1969
After several years of uncertainty, the MOD invites proposals for repurposing the site. Suggestions include a sports centre or a prison.

FEBRUARY 1971
IWM proposes turning Duxford into a museum. Later in the year, IWM is granted temporary permission to store aircraft in the hangars.

1975–PRESENT
De Havilland biplanes at a 1975 air show (left). Duxford opens to the public, as a permanent IWM site, in 1976.
© MARTIN GARNETT

AIR SHOWS AND EVENTS

One of the things that makes IWM Duxford so special is that it is a working airfield. As you walk around the site, especially in the summer months, you can watch Spitfires, Mustangs, Hurricanes, Hellcats and many other aircraft soaring, twisting and swooping in the skies above. It is a powerful experience – the pulse of propellers, the roar of engines, the smell of oil can all transport you back to what the airfield must have been like as a Second World War fighter base.

Air shows (above and right)
Every year Duxford plays host to a programme of air shows and events, featuring aircraft based at the airfield and many more from around the world – historic and current, military and civilian. For the latest information about our air shows, please visit iwm.org.uk.
IWM 2010_043_032; IWM_SITE_DUX_000672;
IWM_SITE_DUX_001369

Flying partners (left)
IWM does not fly any historic aircraft at Duxford, but it has partner organisations who do. The Old Flying Machine Company, the Fighter Collection and the Historic Aircraft Collection all take part in the air shows. And visitors can enjoy a range of thrilling pleasure flights in de Havilland Tiger Moths and Dragon Rapides (see left) operated by Classic Wings. You don't even need to book in advance – just visit the **Classic Wings** office at Duxford. See iwm.org.uk/duxford for more details.
© CLASSIC WINGS

Flying aircraft up close (left)

In **Flying Aircraft** you can see an ever-changing selection of war birds, owned by our partner organisations, being maintained and repaired for a new season of air shows. Here, an engineer works on the Supermarine Mk V Spitfire EP120, owned by The Fighter Collection. Fully restored in 1995, she has been a popular performer in air shows ever since.

IWM_SITE_DUX_001670

Famous aircraft (left)

Many of the privately owned aircraft at Duxford have appeared in films and on television. Perhaps the most famous is 'Sally B', currently the only airworthy Boeing B-17 Flying Fortress in Europe. It featured in the hit 1990 film *Memphis Belle*, which was loosely based on the exploits of a B-17 bomber crew towards the end of the Second World War.

IWM_SITE_DUX_001673

IN THEIR OWN WORDS – CLIFF SPINK, SPITFIRE DISPLAY PILOT

Former RAF officer Air Marshal Cliff Spink (right) has been a display pilot for around 25 years, flying out of Duxford for most of that time. Here he talks about what makes the site so special.

Air shows are like flying museums – the exhibits literally take to the skies. You get such a vibrant experience – especially at Duxford, where you can enjoy the best of both worlds. There are so many wonderful exhibits to look at in detail on the ground, and then you can walk outside to see actual examples flying overhead. It's an enormously powerful combination.

The Duxford Air Show, of course, is famous for its closely choreographed displays. It's all done in a very responsible, professional and carefully controlled way. It's something we pride ourselves on. PHOTOGRAPH © CLIFF SPINK

FLYING AT DUXFORD

During the museum's opening hours a small team of Flight Information Service Officers provides flight information to pilots based at IWM Duxford, and to pilots flying in and out of the historic airfield. For essential information, including instructions to follow in order to fly into the airfield, visit iwm.org.uk/duxford.

AIRSPACE

Next to the entrance to IWM Duxford stands AirSpace — the vast home to our award-winning exhibition about the history and technology of aviation, together with a breathtaking display of over 30 military and civil aircraft.

AirSpace tells the story of aviation in Britain and the Commonwealth, but its first-floor exhibition starts with an exhibit from across the Atlantic — a piece of fabric from the Wright Flyer, the aircraft that achieved the world's first powered, sustained and controlled flight.

From there you can move on to a series of interactive exhibits that explain concepts such as lift and thrust, and what counts as an aircraft at all. Running alongside this is a timeline covering a century and more of aviation history.

Stretching out to your right is the main expanse of the exhibition, where you can get up close to aircraft, engines and weaponry that embody the way that aviation has evolved. This section of the guidebook shows how these exhibits (marked in bold text throughout) fit into the overall story.

Treasure trove (left)
Aircraft from every era fill the exhibition space, and can be viewed from the first-floor walk-way or at ground level, where you can even get beneath the bomb bay of a Vulcan.
IWM_SITE_DUX_001656

'It is not really necessary to look too far into the future; we see enough already to be certain it will be magnificent.'

Wilbur Wright on the possibilities of aviation, 1908

23

DID YOU KNOW?

Some of the most important aviation pioneers were British. George Cayley, for example, designed a man-carrying glider which successfully left the ground for 130m (423 feet) in 1853 — 50 years before the Wright Flyer took to the air.

1903 – 1918: FROM FIRST FLIGHT TO FIRST WORLD WAR

The Wright Flyer made its breakthrough flight in December 1903, and by 1908 the aircraft was being manufactured at Britain's first aeroplane factory. Then, two years later, the country's first 'private pilot licence' was issued, followed by another 49 before the end of the year.

As the idea of manned flight took hold, the military were quick to see its potential, and in 1912 the Royal Flying Corps (RFC) was set up. Initially comprising separate Naval and Military Wings, two years later the Royal Naval Air Service was formed, leaving the RFC as the aviation arm of the British Army.

When war came in 1914 the action on the Western Front quickly descended into a trench-bound stalemate, with artillery used to pound the enemy lines. To begin with, the RFC's main role was to carry out reconnaissance missions on possible targets for shelling, but aircraft such as the **Royal Aircraft**

Factory RE8, which entered service in 1916, proved vulnerable to attack. The fighting scout, later simply the 'fighter', was therefore developed to protect them. Aircraft were also used for bombing raids, which by 1918 went beyond the enemy lines. British pilots, some of whom were trained at Duxford, flew bombers such as the **de Havilland DH9** to carry out these groundbreaking strategic raids.

War had come to the skies, and it fuelled an aviation revolution. At the start of the war Britain had fewer than 150 aeroplanes. By the end it had over 22,000. So integral was air power to the war effort that in 1918 Britain established the Royal Air Force – the world's first independent air force, free from army and navy control.

Early armed aircraft (left)
A de Havilland DH9 is one of the oldest aircraft on display in AirSpace.
IWM_SITE_DUX_001576

Services not required (right)
The Royal Aircraft Factory RE8 in AirSpace – here shown on exterior display – was delivered to the RAF on the very same day that the First World War ended.
IWM 2010.250.2

HISTORY OF AVIATION TIMELINE

In 1903 American brothers Wilbur and Orville Wright became the first to achieve sustained, powered, controlled flight. Since then aviation has progressed at a rapid pace, with many developments fuelled by the imperative of war. Here are some of the key moments in the history of flight – both civil and military.

1910

The first passenger airship, the Zeppelin LZ7, makes its maiden flight in Germany. Such airships would be used to drop bombs over Britain in the First World War.

1917–1919

Construction of Duxford begins in 1917. It operates as No. 35 Training Depot Station (1918–19), to reopen as No. 2 Flying Training School in 1920.

IN THEIR OWN WORDS – FRANK BURSLEM, DH9 PILOT

The First World War saw 'strategic bombing' used for the first time in combat. Here Frank Burslem of 218 Squadron recalls flying his de Havilland DH9 bomber on a raid against a German submarine base:

When we crossed over enemy lines we came under very intense [anti-aircraft] fire and over the target it seemed to increase. We scarcely ever saw a German [aeroplane] but there was one occasion when we had dropped our bombs and were on our way home, I saw the aeroplanes in front of me weaving all over the place, so I started to weave too. And eventually we got back into formation and went back to our base...

And when we were making out our reports, the leader of my formation asked: 'Did you see that Hun on your tail?' And I said: 'No'. And he said: 'Well there was one and you would have been cold meat if I hadn't turned and chased him off!' So I turned to my observer and said: 'Did you see that Hun?' He said: 'No, I was being sick in my cockpit'. And I said: 'You report ill!' and I never flew with him again!

First World War bomber
Aeroplanes like this de Havilland DH9 were among the first to be flown from Duxford airfield in 1918.
IWM Q56858

'You would have been cold meat if I hadn't turned and chased him off!'

DID YOU KNOW?
The First World War was not the first time that an aeroplane was used over a battlefield. In October 1911 a pilot of the Italian Air Flotilla flew a reconnaissance mission over Turkish lines in the year-long Italo-Turkish War.

1919
The world's first regular aeroplane passenger service begins in Germany. Five years later Britain's first national airline, Imperial Airways, is founded.

1935
As tensions in Europe escalate, new monoplane fighters are developed such as the Messerschmitt Bf109 and the Hawker Hurricane (right). IWM CM 131

1939–1945
The Second World War sees long-range bombing campaigns and airborne assaults, plus the advent of the jet engine, radar, flying bomb and rocket.

1919 – 1945: NEW ROUTES AND NEW MILITARY AIRCRAFT

The aircraft industry that exploded into existence during the First World War – including such illustrious names as Sopwith, A.V. Roe and Bristol – shrank in the post-war period. But aeroplanes were here to stay, and new benchmarks were set for distance, height, endurance and reliability in the 1920s and 1930s.

In the late 1920s there also emerged a golden era of high-class, luxurious passenger travel, following the establishment of airlines such as Imperial Airways. The introduction of flying boats like the Short Empire opened up routes to far-flung destinations such as Egypt, South Africa and Australia.

But it was war – or the threat of it – that spurred a new wave of development. In 1933 a belligerent Adolf Hitler became Germany's leader and soon declared his intention to leave the League of Nations, set up in 1919 to settle international disputes without the need for war. The question of Britain's national defence became a priority once more.

26

The remainder of the decade therefore saw the development of new military aircraft such as the **Short Sunderland** (derived from the Short Empire), **Avro Anson**, **Fairey Swordfish**, **Westland Lysander** and **Supermarine Spitfire**, as well as training aircraft like the **Airspeed Oxford** and **Miles Magister**.

The Second World War brought an acceleration to this development. Between 1939 and 1945 Britain welcomed over a million people into its flying armed forces, and the aviation industry grew exponentially.

Over 130,000 aircraft were produced in Britain, the Empire and the Commonwealth during the war, including bombers like the **de Havilland Mosquito** and the **Avro Lancaster** and **York**. They proved vital to the eventual Allied victory.

The Ox-Box (above)

The Airspeed Oxford, nicknamed the 'Ox-Box', was flown by the RAF between 1937 and 1954. It was used to train pilots on twin-engine aircraft who had passed their initial training on single-engine aircraft.
IWM_SITE_DUX_001665

The Swordfish (above)

Between 1936 and 1945 the Fairey Swordfish operated mainly from Royal Navy aircraft carriers. Its roles varied from flying reconnaissance missions to attacking ships (carrying a torpedo or mines) and mounting bombing raids against land targets.
IWM A 3532

1947

The sound barrier is broken for the first time when pilot Charles 'Chuck' Yeager (right) flies the Bell X1 above Mach 1 (the speed of sound). IWM FRE 3128

1950 – 1953

During the Korean War, fighters of the Second World War era give way to new jets such as the Russian MiG15 and the American F86 Sabre.

1957

The 'space race' begins when Sputnik, the first satellite, is launched into space by the Soviet Union. The first human sets foot on the moon 12 years later.

EXHIBIT IN FOCUS: AVRO LANCASTER MK X

After the evacuation of its troops from France in 1940, the only way for Britain to strike at Germany was from the air. But the RAF's bombers did not have the range, capacity or accuracy to inflict serious strategic damage.

In 1942 the Lancaster and Halifax entered service. Now, night after night, Bomber Command could reach far into Germany, and drop much heavier loads of bombs. Together with daytime raids by the United States Army Air Forces, this prolonged assault gradually eroded Germany's ability to sustain its war effort.

Close-knit crew (above)

In the early hours of 6 January 1944, Flying Officer A E Manning and his crew of No. 9 Squadron RAF gather by their Lancaster after raiding Stettin, Germany. The Lancaster's crew of seven comprised the pilot and flight engineer, in the cockpit, with the navigator and wireless operator behind them. In the nose was the bomb aimer, who also manned the front turret gun. The most isolated crew were the mid upper turret and rear turret gunners. IWM CH 11972

IWM 2010_020_3_1

On the nose (left)
Three miles from the target, the bomb aimer would take over from the navigator to direct the pilot towards the aiming position – lying on his stomach and looking through the large circular perspex blister at the front.
IWM_SITE_DUX_001665

'Corkscrew. Port. Go!'

Donald Falgate, a Lancaster bomb aimer, recalls being intercepted by a night fighter close to target:

He caught us with his first burst... We were all ok... so we continued... to the target... He missed us [the second time] and then positioned himself... for his third run...

Our rear gunner screamed out 'Corkscrew. Port. Go!' which was the standard evasive action... down to the left, climbing to the right, down to the left... and fortunately we managed to evade him...

I managed to complete the bombing run... but it was quite frightening...

1946–PRESENT: THE AGE OF THE JET

After the Second World War the aviation industry switched attention to the potential of air travel, with many military aircraft adapted to carry passengers. Turboprop passenger aeroplanes were introduced, followed by jet-powered airliners like the **de Havilland Comet** in the 1950s.

In the 1960s the industry slimmed down and firms merged to form new 'super' companies. Britain still played its part, most notably in the development of the **British Aircraft Corporation/Aerospatiale Concorde** in the 1970s.

There were also post-war developments in military aviation as a new Cold War evolved between East and West, bringing with it the terrible threat of nuclear weapons. The RAF was effectively on the front line of this war, its 'V-bombers' – the **Avro Vulcan**, **Handley Page Victor** and **Vickers Valiant** – carrying Britain's nuclear deterrent, and its jet fighters like the **English Electric Lightning** ready to intercept Soviet bombers.

As military aircraft became more complex (acting as both fighters and bombers, for example), companies joined forces to develop new machines. In the 1960s came the **Sepecat Jaguar**, in the 1980s the **Panavia Tornado**, and this century the **Eurofighter Typhoon** was developed.

Today, after over a century of rich heritage, aircraft remain an integral part of military and civilian life in Britain and the Commonwealth. It is an evolving story that Duxford's **AirSpace** will continue to tell for years to come.

IN THEIR OWN WORDS – NIGEL 'SHARKEY' WARD, HARRIER PILOT

IWM MH 27599

Nigel 'Sharkey' Ward was a Harrier pilot in the Falklands Conflict in 1982. Here he recalls the difficulties of mastering the 'jump jet' technology that made the Harrier unique...

Putting a Phantom or Hunter down on a runway could be done virtually blindfolded, but for any form of landing in the Harrier full concentration was needed. There were strict limitations to be observed... when transitioning from wing-borne flight to jet-borne flight i.e. to the hover.

Going outside those limits could mean ... the jet turning upside down involuntarily. You had to be extremely lucky to survive such a loss of control during an approach to land!

'You had to be extremely lucky to survive such a loss of control!'

1958

The Boeing 707 comes into service. Twice the capacity of other passenger aircraft, its speed heralds the arrival of the jet air travel age.

1967

The Harrier 'jump jet' goes into service with the RAF – the only successful aircraft to use Vertical or Short Take-Off and Landing technology.

1976

The British Aircraft Corporation/Aerospatiale Concorde (left) goes into service with BA – the only airliner to fly at over twice the speed of sound.

IWM MH 22884

Fighters then and now (above)
A Eurofighter Typhoon and a
Spitfire fly alongside each other at
the Duxford 75th anniversary Battle
of Britain air show in 2015.
IWM 2015_079_0373

1983
The first stealth aircraft,
the Lockheed F-117, enters
service with the USAF. This
precision attack aircraft is
almost invisible to radar.

1991
The Gulf War begins after
Iraqi forces invade Kuwait.
It sees the introduction
of stealth technology and
precision 'smart' weapons to
the battlefield.

2001
The MQ1 Predator
becomes the first
Unmanned Aerial Vehicle,
commonly known as a
'drone', to be used in a
combat role.

2016
IWM Duxford's American
Air Museum reopens after
a major redevelopment
programme, to explore
US air power in the 20th
and 21st centuries.

AIR AND SEA

As an island nation, Britain largely used to base its defences on control of the sea. This changed during the First World War, when German airships mounted the first ever bombing raids over British towns and cities. Since then Britain's air and sea forces have had to work in ever closer cooperation – countering threats above and below the waves, and developing new offensive capabilities to carry the fight to the enemy. This is the evolution explored in Air and Sea.

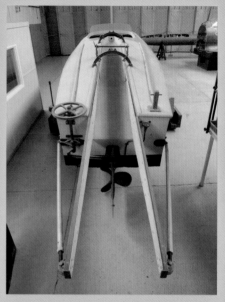

Coastal Motor Boat (right)
The torpedo changed the nature of naval warfare during and after the First World War. It made warships vulnerable to attack from newly developed submarines and from much smaller surface ships.

Designed with a rear-facing trough to carry a single torpedo, this Coastal Motor Boat (CMB 4) was ordered by the Admiralty from British shipbuilding company, J I Thornycroft, in 1916. CMB 4 was the boat commanded by Lieutenant Augustus Agar (see below) when the Russian cruiser *Oleg* was sunk. For his actions on that day in June 1919, Agar was awarded the Victoria Cross.

IWM_SITE_DUX_001674

IN THEIR OWN WORDS – LIEUTENANT AUGUSTUS AGAR VC

During the night of 17 June 1919 Lieutenant Augustus Agar carried out a daring attack on a Russian cruiser *Oleg*, as part of a British intervention in the Russian Civil War. He evaded mines and enemy ships to steer his Coastal Motor Boat to within 1,000 yards of the Bolshevik-held cruiser. Here he remembers the scene after he fired his torpedo.

Unfortunately I had been seen ... and had drawn the fire of everything on all sides ... There was hardly time to think or look. I had to concentrate on my boat which, now going at high speed, was sufficient protection against the firing ... I could hear the shells whistling overhead – and it's not very pleasant when they splash and one has to send the boat through the column of water...

But we got away, and I looked behind and I saw... a large column of smoke almost as high as the mast of the ship... and a big red flash. There was no doubt about it – I had hit the target.

IWM Q 114301

Biber No. 90

In the Second World War German submarines sank thousands of Allied merchant ships, starving Britain of supplies. Churchill later admitted that the 'U-boat peril' was the one thing that really frightened him during the war. The smallest submarine in the German Navy was the Biber (beaver), which was operated by only one crewman. It proved to be largely ineffectual against the Allies, due to technical flaws and poorly trained crews. The example on display is Biber No. 90, which was found sinking 49 miles north-east of Dover on 29 December 1944. IWM MAR_000558

Fairey Gannet (right) and Hawker Siddeley Buccaneer (far right)

The Second World War saw the coming of age of the aircraft carrier, equipped with aircraft able to operate reconnaissance missions and strike at targets well beyond the reach of land-based aeroplanes. Today, only helicopter carriers are used.

There are several examples in Air and Sea of aircraft designed for use on board carriers – from the 1957 Fairey Gannet to the Hawker Siddeley Buccaneer jet.

IWM_SITE_DUX_001573
IWM_SITE_DUX_001572

BATTLE OF BRITAIN

The Battle of Britain exhibition shows how Britain's air defences evolved from the First World War through to the jet age. At its heart is the Battle of Britain itself – the momentous aerial campaign of 1940. This section of the guidebook tells the story of the battle and the role played in it by the fighter squadrons of RAF Duxford.

On 10 May 1940 Hitler launched a sudden offensive on the Western Front. A few shocking days later his armies had burst through the Allied lines and, within two weeks, Duxford's 19 and 264 Squadrons had been ordered south to cover the evacuation of British troops from the coastline around the French port of Dunkirk. They flew dozens of sorties between 26 May and 1 June, with several pilots killed or becoming prisoners of war.

Britain now faced the threat of invasion. It was a danger brought home to Duxford by night-time bombing raids carried out by the Luftwaffe. The airfield itself escaped with a few near misses, but the sound of anti-aircraft batteries became commonplace and reports were rife of damage and loss of life in nearby towns and villages.

To guarantee the success of the invasion, Hitler wanted to establish air superiority over southern England. So began what would become known as the Battle of Britain – a battle that the RAF's Fighter Command simply had to win if Britain was to survive.

'Never in the field of human conflict was so much owed by so many to so few.'

Prime Minister Winston Churchill, on the air crew standing between Britain and a German invasion, 20 August 1940

33

Back to Blighty (far left)
The **Spitfire** on display in the exhibition was based at Duxford before the Battle of Britain. It crash-landed on a French beach in May 1940. In 1986 it was discovered and restored, and it was donated to IWM Duxford in 2014.
IWM_SITE_DUX_001571

10 JULY – 11 AUGUST: THE BATTLE BEGINS

The Luftwaffe had been targeting Allied shipping since the start of the war, threatening Britain's vital supply lines of oil, food, ships and weapons. After the fall of France these attacks became heavier and more frequent — especially in the English Channel. The biggest and most sustained of these came on 10 July, a date now regarded as the first day of the Battle of Britain.

It was Fighter Command's job to mount a defence against these attacks. Its forces were organised into four groups: 10 Group looked after the south-west; 11 Group the south-east (including London); 12 Group (which included RAF Duxford) the Midlands; and 13 Group the north.

In these first few weeks of the battle, therefore, the bulk of the work was carried out by the pilots of 11 Group. The men of 12 Group flew plenty of sorties, but only came into sporadic contact with the enemy.

34

12 – 23 AUGUST: THE ACTION INTENSIFIES

On 12 August the Luftwaffe launched a systematic assault on the RAF's forward airfields and radar stations. It heralded the beginning of *Adlerangriff* (Eagle Attack) — considered in Germany to be the true start of the battle. The aim of the campaign was summed up with brutal simplicity by Reichsmarschall Hermann Goering, Commander in Chief of the Luftwaffe. It was to 'wipe the British Air Force from the sky'.

Hundreds of German bombers and fighters joined in attacks to the south on 12 and 13 August. Then, two days later, Goering made use of all three of his available Air Fleets, sending thousands of aircraft to probe the RAF's defences up and down the land.

DID YOU KNOW?

In wartime Britain it was cheaper and quicker to produce a new aeroplane than it was to train a new pilot. At one point in the battle, Fighter Command considered itself 200 flyers short of what it needed.

Pressure of work (left)
19 Squadron pilot Brian 'Sandy' Lane stares into the camera after a day of heavy combat in September 1940. He is flanked by Walter 'Farmer' Lawson (left) and George 'Grumpy' Unwin (right).
IWM CH 1366

BATTLE OF BRITAIN TIMELINE

In 1941 the Air Ministry published *The Battle of Britain*, a pamphlet dating the battle as 8 August to 31 September 1940. This was later broadened by the Air Ministry to the dates we use today —10 July to 31 October. This timeline covers the most significant days of the battle as a whole, and for the men and women of RAF Duxford in particular.

10 JULY

On what is now considered to be the opening day of the Battle of Britain, the Luftwaffe begins by targeting British convoys in the English Channel.

16 JULY

Hitler issues a directive for a landing in Britain — an invasion for which the Luftwaffe is expected to clear the way.

EXHIBIT IN FOCUS: MESSERSCHMITT Bf 109E-3 (Me 109E)

The Luftwaffe flew Messerschmitt 109 fighter planes during the Battle of Britain in 1940.

With a top speed of 354mph (570kph) – and able to operate from a maximum height of 36,091ft (11,000m) – the 109 could outperform the RAF's Hurricanes, and was even a match for the Spitfire.

However, it only had a range of 412 miles (663km), which reduced the time it could spend over England. This limitation proved to be crucial to the outcome of the battle.

Captured for posterity (above)
The Messerschmitt 109 on display in the Battle of Britain exhibition crash-landed near East Dean in Sussex on 30 September 1940. Its pilot, Horst Perez, was captured and the aircraft was placed under armed guard (above).

IWM HU 73139

IWM 2010_200_1

Hidden detail (below)
In some areas you can see names scratched into the paintwork of the Messerschmitt 109 on display. After its capture it went on a tour of North America to raise money for Britain's war effort; contributors could leave their mark. When IWM acquired the aircraft in 1998 parts were painted over with a removable water-based paint, making the names less visible. IWM_SITE_DUX_001569

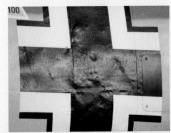

John Hills was nine when he witnessed the Messerschmitt's pilot Horst Perez being taken prisoner. Here he recalls the scene:

A lady in front of me... asked him what he thought about being a prisoner of war... He replied that he was not too concerned as the war would be over soon and he would be released – something that was taken to imply that he expected the invasion to take place shortly and that he would be on the winning side.

'...he expected the invasion to take place shortly ...'

24 AUGUST –
6 SEPTEMBER: PUSHED
TO THE LIMITS

A long way from home (above)
Pilots of 310 (Czech) Squadron relax at Duxford in September 1940. Six of them did not survive the war.
IWM CH 1299

Poor weather brought a lull in the battle between 19 and 23 August. When hostilities resumed the Luftwaffe changed tactics, sending over fewer bombers and more fighters, and concentrating their fire on industrial targets and the airfields of 11 Group.

Faced with so many escort fighters, the British struggled to stop the bombers reaching their targets. Over the coming days six of 11 Group's seven sector stations suffered heavy damage. Duxford escaped the bombs, but Fowlmere was hit on 31 August. Despite the ever-increasing strain on resources, Fighter Command managed to repair its airfields and had temporary Ops Rooms at the ready. Everyone, however – pilots and ground crews alike – could feel the pressure building.

Credit for victory in the Battle of Britain is often given to the 'few' – the pilots who took the fight directly to the Luftwaffe. It was thanks to the 'many' – the thousands of flight trainers and factory workers, the repair crews and the ground staff – that by 6 September Fighter Command could call upon over 200 more pilots and 150 more aeroplanes than at the start of the battle (while the Luftwaffe's total number of pilots was decreasing).

It was a remarkable feat that the Luftwaffe couldn't match. It also led the Germans to underestimate Fighter Command's resources; they thought that it would take only one or two more massive engagements to finish off the British.

12 AUGUST
The Luftwaffe launches a systematic day-time assault on the RAF's forward airfields and radar stations, involving hundreds of bombers and fighters.

13 AUGUST
'Eagle Day' – regarded by the Germans as the true start of the battle. The RAF's defences are probed by 1,485 German sorties over a period of 10 hours.

15 AUGUST
The Luftwaffe deploys its three air fleets together for the first time. It is the heaviest day of fighting in the whole battle, from the south coast to Scotland.

17 AUGUST
The first Czech Squadron – number 310 – becomes operational and starts flying patrols from Duxford.

7 SEPTEMBER: CHANGE OF TACTICS

By the start of September, 12 Group was instructed to protect 11 Group's airfields during attacks. Keen to concentrate his forces to hit the enemy hard, Air Vice Marshal Trafford Leigh-Mallory, 12 Group's Commander, arranged for 19, 242 and 310 Squadrons to fly together out of Duxford as a wing under the leadership of Douglas Bader. Later this 'Duxford Wing' comprised up to five squadrons.

Not everyone agreed with this approach. Although the wing had strength in numbers and did meet with some success, it did not always get to where 11 Group needed it, sometimes leaving its airfields open to attack. This caused tension between the Groups, but either way Duxford's pilots were soon able to see plenty of action. At 4pm on 7 September a German force of 300 bombers and 600 fighters was picked up heading for Kent and Sussex. By 5pm Duxford's 19, 242 and 310 squadrons were all in the air, together with many of 11 Group's units. Soon they were in position to thwart the expected raids on airfields across the south-east.

But these separate raids didn't come. Instead every German aeroplane continued on to London, where the bombers laid waste to the docks before the British fighters could intercept them. A second wave of bombers enjoyed similar success, sparking huge fires in East London that lit the way for further raids overnight. The Blitz had begun.

The raid was so successful that the Germans believed the RAF was close to finished. A week later they were ready to deliver the killer blow.

IN THEIR OWN WORDS – SPITFIRE PILOT GEORGE 'GRUMPY' UNWIN

Back on the ground
George Unwin climbs out of his Supermarine Spitfire – this time after a safer kind of landing.
IWM CH 1355

On 11 September George 'Grumpy' Unwin, of Duxford's 19 Squadron, was on a sortie when he caught sight of a lone Dornier bomber heading back towards the English Channel. Following the usual drill he first took aim at the rear gunner...

I gave him a burst and shut him up. At least I thought I had... because as I closed right in... I suddenly saw his rear gunner shooting back at me... Suddenly I was covered in smoke... I was leaning forward of course, as one did, to the gun-sight and a hole appeared in this thing in front of my face. I thought, 'Good God, I must be dead or something...' – I thought I was on fire.

So I whipped the hood back, undid my straps and... was halfway out of the cockpit when I suddenly saw that [the] smoke was coming from the top of the engine, through the engine cowling, which is where the glycol [coolant] pipe is... So I strapped myself in again, left the hood open... went rapidly down-hill... and then started looking for a field... I got down to about 1,000 feet, dropped the undercarriage and did a forced landing... no trouble at all.

---

18 AUGUST
The Germans fly some 750 sorties, but sustain so much damage that the Ju 87 dive bomber (right) is rarely seen again during the battle. IWM GER 18

30 AUGUST
The RAF flies 1,054 sorties – its busiest day in the battle so far. More than 20 squadrons, including Duxford's, have to make up to four sorties each.

31 AUGUST
The Germans target RAF Sector Stations, including Duxford. The RAF suffers it costliest day yet, losing 39 aircraft and 14 pilots

IN THEIR OWN WORDS – BATTLE OF BRITAIN FIGHTER PILOTS

Douglas Bader (right) played a key role during the battle as leader of a 'Big Wing' of up to five squadrons. Here he recalls the contrasting hours spent on the ground and in the air...

You spent probably three or four or five hours in the air [in a 24-hour period]... an hour at a time or an hour and a half. Tremendous exhilaration, you know, tremendous excitement.

And [in between] you were sat out there in the sunshine, eating or drinking tea or coffee or something, or playing the gramophone, the ones you used to wind up, you know, playing cards. Long hours of boredom....

On 31 August 1940 Duxford experienced one of its busiest days of the battle. Here David Cox gives a sense of the dangers that he and the other Spitfire pilots faced...

These 110s came down very, very quickly. And we turned into them [but] old Coward went straight on then he got hit... He obviously hadn't seen them... Frankie Brinsden, he was attacked... and had to bail out and Coward was hit and bailed out... he lost his foot. Young Aeberhardt [was] hit and coming in to land... the thing turned over... I remember coming in to land over his burning wreckage.

IWM CH 1405

'People you'd been having breakfast with didn't come back at 11 o'clock.'

Spitfire pilot Richard Jones thought that Bader's 'Big Wing' could take too long to form up and engage the enemy, but he later decided that the advantages outweighed the disadvantages...

I think it brought the turning point psychologically in the battle... You looked around you and saw 65 to 70 Spitfires and Hurricanes... It gave you terrific confidence.... And I think... when the Germans [saw it] for the first time... it put the fear of God up them.

Douglas Bader describes how to cope when pilots didn't make it back to base...

You lived very much on the surface. If you took it to heart when people you'd been having breakfast with didn't come back at 11 o'clock, you could never have got on... You aren't any the less conscious of losing something, but... one has got to get on with the job.

You have this protective skin – what one calls understatement – which is in the British character... and it's easily acquired.

---

6 SEPTEMBER
Douglas Bader and 242 Squadron begin operating as part of the 'Duxford Wing' alongside 310 and 19 Squadrons.

7 SEPTEMBER
In a change of tactics the Luftwaffe targets London to lure the RAF into a massive, decisive air battle. It is the start of a nine-month 'Blitz' on the city (right). IWM C 5422

9 SEPTEMBER
Bader's Wing flies over London in pursuit of enemy bombers. Along with 11 Group planes, they claim to have shot down 21 enemy aircraft.

15 SEPTEMBER: DAY OF RECKONING

By 11am on 15 September German aeroplanes were massing over the French coast. Anticipating another raid on London, Fighter Command concentrated its aircraft in huge numbers. Just the day before, for example, it had added an extra two squadrons to Bader's Duxford Wing.

The Germans approached with no attempt at surprise – there were no feints or diversionary ploys. They were confident that the day would end with a decisive victory. And they were right.

The incoming bombers and fighters came over in two distinct waves – one at 11.30am and one at 2pm. At RAF Duxford and across southern England fighters formed up to meet the first wave, returned to refuel and rearm, and then had time to take off again to meet the second raid. Some of the German formations were split apart, others took heavy damage and incurred heavy losses.

By the end of the day – now commemorated as Battle of Britain Day – it was obvious that the Luftwaffe were no closer to delivering the air supremacy required to support an invasion. Two days later Hitler gave the order for the landing operation to be postponed.

Bigger and better? (above)
Part of the Duxford 'Big Wing' can be seen here heading into battle. Argument continues to this day over its effectiveness.
IWM CH 1429

DID YOU KNOW?

Douglas Bader – the most famous pilot to fly from Duxford during the war – lost both his legs in a flying accident in 1931. Determined to fly again, he eventually convinced the RAF to let him rejoin the force in 1939 and went on to fight with distinction.

16 SEPTEMBER – 31 OCTOBER: FROM BATTLE TO BLITZ

After 15 September bombing raids continued, but by October the defences of Fighter Command were no longer seriously under threat. There were no more concerted attacks on airfields, and daylight raids dwindled. The Duxford Wing, for example, flew 19 patrols between 19 September and 31 October, but only saw significant action once on 27 September, when two pilots were killed and one wounded.

However, the nightly bombing raids that first came on 7 September continued. This Blitz would carry on for nine months, killing thousands of civilians and causing terrible damage. Fighter Command had thwarted the planned German invasion, but it would be almost five years before the possibility of defeat would be completely extinguished.

15 SEPTEMBER	17 SEPTEMBER	18 SEPTEMBER	31 OCTOBER
On what is later known as 'Battle of Britain Day', the Duxford Wing is in action twice, helping to see off huge German raids.	The setback suffered on 15 September proves decisive, as Hitler postpones his planned invasion of Britain until further notice.	The Duxford Wing intercepts bombers heading up the Thames towards London, shooting down a number of German aeroplanes.	Over a period of weeks the Luftwaffe switches slowly to night-time raids. The Battle of Britain comes to an end.

1940 OPERATIONS ROOM

The Operations Room was the nerve centre of RAF Duxford during the Battle of Britain. It was here that information on enemy aircraft was gathered and plotted on the map, and instructions were issued to the pilots scrambling to meet any incoming threat.

Flying colours (above)
The Operations Room clock. Every time a report about enemy aircraft came in, the plotters flagged it up on the map as red, yellow or blue, depending on which five-minute segment of the hour was indicated on the clock.
IWM_SITE_DUX_001568

Sights and sounds of war (below)
Our curators have reconstructed the Operations Room as it would have appeared during the Battle of Britain, complete with a soundtrack based on a German air attack that took place on 31 August 1940.
IWM DUX 331

The original room (right)

This photograph of the Operations Room was taken on 19 September 1940. Sitting in the centre of the raised dais was the Controller – the most senior officer in the room. It was his job to talk Duxford's fighters into the best possible position to intercept enemy raids.

To his left was an Army Liaison Officer and two signallers, who made sure that any anti-aircraft fire was coordinated with the efforts of the pilots. Below was a Floor Supervisor who oversaw the work of the Plotters. Other officers not shown in the photograph were in touch with the airfield at Duxford and at nearby Fowlmere, as well as the headquarters of 12 Group at Watnall. Others were responsible for keeping track of where the Duxford pilots were, and for calculating the interception courses that they needed to fly.

At the height of a raid new reports could be coming in every few seconds, and the voices of pilots in the thick of the action could be heard coming through over the radio. Tension was high, but concentration and calm efficiency was vital.

IWM CH 1401

IN THEIR OWN WORDS – JEAN MILLS, OPERATIONS ROOM PLOTTER

Jean Mills was a member of the Women's Auxiliary Air Force (WAAF). She worked in the Operations Room at RAF Duxford, receiving reports on enemy aircraft movements and plotting them on the map. Here she recalls the thrill – and shock – of her arrival at the base one hot summer's day in August 1940...

So there we were about a dozen of us clinging on to the sides [of an open-backed lorry] and laughing and talking and really quite excited. Of course we were all pretty young,18 or 19 I suppose, and most of us hadn't been away from home before and life was a great adventure.

We reached the brow of a hill and we could see Duxford stretched out before us... There had obviously been something going on because planes seemed to be landing from all directions. And as we looked one appeared to hover for a moment and then it nose-dived straight down into the ground... And I think we then realised that it wasn't a great lark, it was serious business that we were in for.

Back on the ground

Four WAAF plotters pose for a photograph in the RAF Duxford Operations Room, 1940.

IWM CH 1404

AMERICAN AIR MUSEUM

The American Air Museum tells the story of the collaboration betwen Britain and America in war. It focuses on how American air power has played a key part in conflict in the 20th and 21st centuries.

The development of aviation in the United States was driven by the country's entry into the First World War in April 1917.

At first, the pilots of the US Army Air Service flew aircraft manufactured by British, French or Italian companies. All but one of the 16 US fighter squadrons that served on the Western Front, for example, were equipped with the French-made **Spad XIII**.

By 1918 the US had 195,000 airmen operating 3,500 aircraft in Europe. Alongside European-made aircraft, they flew British-designed DH4s made in the US by US companies and equipped with the US Liberty engine.

In the 1920s and 1930s, companies such as Wright, Burgess, Curtiss, Martin, Thomas-Morse and Boeing would play their part in the rapid expansion of American civil aviation. Military aviation, however, lagged behind, with one US general in 1939 describing the American air forces as 'fifth rate'. It took another world war to transform the US into the world's leading air power.

> *'It was the most complete unification of military effort ever achieved by two Allied nations.'*
>
> **US General George C. Marshall on Anglo-American cooperation in the Second World War**

Iconic building (left)
The American Air Museum was designed by the internationally renowned architect Lord Foster. It won the 1998 Stirling Prize for excellence in architecture.
IWM_SITE_DUX_001584

1942–1945:
WAR IN EUROPE

From 1939 to 1945 the United States built some 325,000 aircraft, a total greater than the combined production of Britain, Germany and Japan.

The aircraft built in greater numbers than any other was the **Consolidated B-24 Liberator**, the four-engined heavy bomber used by the US 8th Air Force on daylight raids over Germany and occupied Europe. Together with the better known **B-17 Flying Fortress**, it spearheaded a massive bomber offensive from 1942 through to 1945 that was designed to destroy Germany's war effort.

By the spring of 1944, the US 8th and 9th Air Forces occupied over 120 airfields in the UK, with half a million personnel and over 9,000 aircraft. In 1943 RAF Duxford was itself taken over by the 8th Air Force, and became host to the 82nd, 83rd and 84th Fighter Squadrons of the 78th Fighter Group.

Flying the **Republic P-47 Thunderbolt** and later the **North American P-51 Mustang**, these squadrons were tasked with accompanying the bombers to their targets and fighting off any enemy aircraft. It was a lonely, exhausting experience for the pilots, strapped into a small noisy cockpit for somewhere between three and seven hours at a time.

Bomber crews too had to fly for up to eleven hours in freezing, vibrating, deafening conditions. And every mission was fraught with danger. In the first year of operations, only 36 per cent of heavy bomber airmen had a chance of completing a 25-mission tour.

Together with the US 9th Air Force, which provided support for ground forces in north-west Europe, the 8th Air Force made a decisive contribution to the Allied victory in the war. But the cost was high – over 80,000 Allied airmen and 600,000 German civilians lost their lives.

Superior model (above)
The consolidated B-24M Liberator had a longer range than the earlier B-17 bomber.
© JOHN HUGHES

DID YOU KNOW?
A single day's action for the 8th Air Force in 1944 could involve 20,000 men, 2,000 bombers, 1,000 fighters and up to 59 different airfields.

AMERICAN MILITARY AVIATION TIMELINE
The US is now the world's leading air power, but this was not always the case. This timeline charts the key dates in the development of the country's aerial prowess and the changing role that aviation has played within the US armed services.

APRIL 1916
The US joins the First World War. By 1918 its small Aviation Section, Signal Corps, has been expanded into the United States Army Air Service (USAAS).

JULY 1926
The USAAS is renamed the US Army Air Corps (USAAC). Part of the Army and Navy, it struggles for funding until war breaks out in Europe in 1939.

EXHIBIT IN FOCUS: DOUGLAS C-47A SKYTRAIN (DAKOTA)

The Douglas DC-3, one of the most popular airliners of all time, first flew in 1935. The military version is the C-47A Skytrain (known as the Dakota in RAF service). It owes its success to its toughness, power and stability and – most importantly – to its capacity to carry a 7,500 lb (3,402 kg) cargo or up to 28 equipped troops. It can perform a general transport role, as well as carrying paratroops, evacuating casualties and towing gliders.

The USAAF and the RAF employed around a thousand C-47s each during Operation Overlord on 6 June 1944.

Heading into action (above)
British paratroops of 1st Airborne Division in a Dakota aircraft on their way to Arnhem during Operation Market Garden, 17 September 1944. Over 10,000 C-47s were built and used during the Second World War.

IWM K 7586

© PETER GREEN

The C-47 at Duxford was manufactured in Long Beach California in 1943. It was delivered to the USAAF in April 1944, and served with the 316th Troop Carrier Group of the 9th Air Force. Assigned to the 37th Troop Carrier Squadron, it operated from Cottesmore, Lincolnshire for a year – seeing action in the Normandy Landings, at Arnhem and during the Rhine Crossings.

After the Second World War it was flown by a Swedish airline, and served with the Spanish Air Force until 1980. It was flown in the Duxford Airshow in 1981, and came into the care of IWM later that same year.

James Manning flew Dakotas for the RAF from 1945 to 1949. Here he explains why British pilots recall the 'Uncle Dak' with affection:

It was a gentleman's aeroplane ... You've got to remember that it was designed as a civil aeroplane ... and we converted it into a military aeroplane. It was very comfortable up front on the flight deck ... We had lovely padded seats ... with upholstered arms... and the cockpit heating was good ... Compared with a lot of British aircraft, it looked as if it had been laid out according to a plan!

'It looked as if it had been laid out according to a plan.'

IN THEIR OWN WORDS – P-51 PILOTS HUIE LAMB AND JOHN C CHILDS

On 29 December 1944 Lieutenant Huie Lamb and his wingman, Flight Officer John C Childs, were flying from Duxford on their first mission in the new P-51 Mustang. During the raid over Germany, Childs' radio went out and Lamb was ordered to escort him back to base.

Lieutenant Huie Lamb recalls what happened next...

We were cruising at 25,000 feet when my plane suddenly lost its engine coolant and began losing power. My first thought was to stretch my glide and try to make it back to the English coast, but I was dropping too fast. Then the nose of my plane burst into flames and I decided to bail out. I couldn't release the canopy. I finally got the canopy open but was too low to bail out...

I saw the whitecaps coming up at me. Somehow I was able to point the nose into wind, drop my flaps, and stall out just above the surface. I tried to hit the water as slow as possible.

The tail hit first. Then a wave caught my right wing and the plane cart-wheeled. It was a miracle that I survived the ditching because I had my seat belt and harness unbuckled in anticipation of bailing out. I got out of my seat and out of the plane, pushing away as far as possible to avoid down-suction. The nose plunged under with a burst of steam. The plane sank like a rock. It was gone in thirty seconds.

The water was freezing cold. I pulled the strings to inflate my Mae West and dinghy, but I couldn't get into the dinghy so I just hung on for dear life.

Living to tell the tale
Lamb (face bandaged) and Childs pose for a photograph after Lamb's rescue.
IWM UPL 6608

Flight Officer Childs, who watched Lamb's descent with horror, takes up the story...

I circled around and saw him with his dinghy. I rocked my wings as a signal I was going for help.

I had no radio ... I took a 278 degree heading toward England. Pretty soon I saw a lighthouse at Orford Ness. I dropped to 500 feet and headed inland... It was a cloudy day. Suddenly I spotted [Martlesham Heath] airfield with a big old twin-engined Walrus flying boat of the British Air Rescue sitting there with its engine running.

Another P-51 pilot had seen the incident and had sent a Mayday, so Martlesham Heath were ready to go. Childs led the Walrus to Lamb, who was still clinging to his dinghy. He escaped with a cut lip, broken tooth and hypothermia, and was flying again ten days later.

'A wave caught my right wing and the plane cart-wheeled...'

JUNE 1941
The USAAC becomes the US Army Air Forces (USAAF). By December it is at war, when Japan attacks the US fleet at Pearl Harbor (right).
IWM NYF 22545

1941–1945
In Europe, USAAF bombers and fighter escorts seriously weaken Germany's war machine, and support Allied troops on the ground.

1941–1945
In the Pacific, carrier-based fighters help to defeat the Japanese Navy. Bombers then target mainland Japan. After the use of atom bombs the war comes to an end.

1941 – 1945:
WAR IN THE PACIFIC

The US entered the war after the surprise Japanese attack on the American fleet at Pearl Harbor on 7 December 1941. The subsequent campaign in the Pacific was a clash between the navies of the two countries – and in particular their naval air power.

Carrier-based dive-bombers such as the Japanese Aichi D3A and torpedo aircraft such as the American Grumman TBM-3 Avenger could destroy an enemy at distances far greater than battleships. The US removed the threat of the Japanese navy in a string of victories, mainly decided by aircraft. US Navy carriers then supported a series of amphibious landings to take ground forces island by island across the Pacific.

The new **Boeing B-29 Superfortress** caused devastating damage. Raids started on Japan in June 1944 – flying from bases in India, staging through China and on to Japan. Then, when the Mariana Islands became available from November 1944, the Americans moved their B-29s there. Japan's economy was shattered. Civilian casualties exceeded 800,000, including 300,000 dead; millions became homeless.

On 6 August 1945, a single atomic bomb was dropped by the B-29 Enola Gay on Hiroshima, killing 80,000 people. A second was dropped on Nagasaki on 9 August killing 35,000.

Carrying a threat (below)
The B-25 Mitchell first became famous in April 1942 when sixteen of the aircraft flew from the carrier USS *Hornet* to make a daring raid on Tokyo.
© PETER GREEN

SEPTEMBER 1947
In recognition of its vital strategic role and offensive capability, the USAAF becomes the US Air Force (USAF) – independent of the army and navy.

JUNE 1948
The Soviets block access to West Berlin, attempting to secure control of the entire city. The USAF helps to fly in supplies, and eventually the Soviets back down.

JUNE 1950
Communist North Korea invades UN-backed South Korea. The USAF plays a major part in the war that follows, until the ceasefire of 1953.

OCTOBER 1962
A USAF spy plane reveals Soviet moves to site nuclear missiles in Cuba. The resulting crisis is the closest that the world has come to nuclear war.

1946 – 1989: THE COLD WAR

The atomic bomb ushered in a new nuclear age, characterised by a tense stand-off between the US and the Soviet Union. Given that in the 1940s aircraft were the only means of delivering nuclear bombs, this 'Cold War' soon led to further developments in military aviation. Tellingly, for example, the US Air Force (USAF) became independent of the US Army and Navy in 1947.

One of its first tasks was to take part in the Berlin Airlift in 1948–1949, delivering supplies to West Berlin which had been blockaded by the Soviets in attempt to secure control of the entire city. Then came the Korean War of 1950–1953, which saw American air power used on a massive scale.

In the mid-1950s the US introduced the **Boeing B-52 Stratofortress** – a jet-powered aircraft with such a long range that it was capable of bombing the Soviet Union from bases in the US. By the end of the decade it had more than 1,800 long-range jet bombers, many of which were deployed to bases in Western Europe, including in the UK, and the Far East.

There were advances too in reconnaissance aircraft, with the **Lockheed U-2C** introduced to spy on the Soviet Union and other communist countries. It was a photograph taken by one such aeroplane in 1962 that revealed the installation of medium-range Soviet nuclear missiles on Cuba – within striking distance of the US mainland. The resulting crisis brought the world to the brink of nuclear war.

Despite this scare, the rivalry between the two superpowers continued, fuelling what would become the war in Vietnam. Here though, air power – despite the use of innovative swing-wing combat aircraft such as the **General Dynamics F-111E Aardvark 'F One Eleven'** – did not prove to be a decisive factor.

Record holder (above)
The Lockheed SR-71A Blackbird was a USAF strategic reconnaissance aircraft from 1968 to 1997. It is the fastest manned jet aeroplane.
DUX_2002_019_008

The introduction of long-range nuclear missiles in the 1960s reduced the need for a large bomber force, and during the 1970s and 1980s the USAF NATO commitment was cut back to three fighter-bomber wings and one reconnaissance wing. After the fall of the Berlin Wall in 1989 and the collapse of the Soviet Union, this commitment was reduced still further as the Cold War ended and new threats emerged.

DID YOU KNOW?

The first known lethal strike by an unmanned aerial vehicle or 'drone' took place in Afghanistan in late 2001. Drones have become a defining weapon in the 'war on terror'.

1960–1975

The US provides military support to combat a communist insurrection in South Vietnam. The USAF plays a major but ultimately indecisive role.

NOVEMBER 1989

Communist regimes collapse in Poland and Hungary, and citizens tear down the Berlin Wall – marking the symbolic end of the Cold War.

JANUARY 1991

Coalition forces oust Iraqi invaders from Kuwait. 'Smart' bombs dropped by USAF planes (left) pave the way for a ground war of only 100 hours.
IWM GLF 1110

1990 – PRESENT: INTO A NEW CENTURY

The fall of communism had repercussions that lasted well into the 1990s. The breakup of Yugoslavia, for example, resulted in a humanitarian disaster, which prompted military intervention by USAF forces under the flags of NATO and the UN.

The Middle East also became a new source of concern. In the Gulf War of 1990–91 US forces spearheaded a coalition assembled to liberate Kuwait from its Iraqi invaders. The region has remained unstable ever since, giving rise to global terrorist networks such as al-Qaeda, which mounted attacks on America in September 2001.

The resulting 'war on terror' has seen US and British forces committed to conflicts in Afghanistan, where al-Qaeda was based, and Iraq, due – it was stated – to the potential for nuclear, chemical or biological weapons falling into the hands of terrorists or unfriendly countries. The regimes in both countries have been changed and the leader of al-Qaeda, Osama bin Laden, killed, but the threat of terror remains – with groups such as ISIS (Islamic State of Iraq and Syria) emerging amid years of bitter civil war in the region.

'Counting the Cost'
Outside the American Air Museum stands a memorial by artist Renato Niemis. Each aircraft engraved on its glass panels represents a plane missing in action in operations flown by US air forces from Britain during the Second World War.
IWM_SITE_DUX_001557

1991–1999	**SEPTEMBER 2001**	**MARCH 2003**	**MAY 2011**
As Yugoslavia descends into civil war, USAF planes, flying under NATO colours, take part in campaigns in Bosnia and Herzogovina in 1995 and Kosovo in 1999.	Terrorists crash hijacked aircraft into the World Trade Center and the Pentagon. A month later the USAF is supporting a US-led invasion of Afghanistan.	Air strikes by the USAF herald the start of an invasion of Iraq. Coalition forces, led by the US, go on to oust the country's leader Saddam Hussein.	US forces kill al-Qaeda leader Osama bin Laden in Pakistan. Other groups continue with terrorism, for example ISIS (Islamic State of Iraq and Syria).

CONSERVATION IN ACTION

Every day in **Conservation in Action** you can watch our team of dedicated staff and volunteers caring for a range of extraordinary aircraft, vehicles and other exhibits. During the redevelopment of the American Air Museum, for example, visitors saw our conservators inspecting a steady stream of iconic US aircraft and readying them for display in the newly refurbished space.

A paint job and a half (left)
Conservation Officer Andy Robinson poses with a spray gun during repainting work on the **B-25J Mitchell bomber**. The museum's exhibition team wanted the aircraft to be given a new paint scheme so that it would match a specific plane that served with the USAAF's 488th Bomb Squadron in the Second World War. Three conservation staff spent a period of six weeks working on the project, which relied on painstaking research to make sure that every colour and marking was correct.
IWM_SITE_DUX_001646

Heavy lifting (right)
Conservation staff Harmon King (ex USAF) and Gordon Turner (ex RAF) remove one of eight 2.5-ton solid-filling wheels from beneath the museum's **B-52 bomber**, in preparation for fitting the aircraft with pneumatic tyres. The job required the use of a jack capable of supporting 50 tons of weight.
IWM_SITE_DUX_001648

Friends reunited (right)

Members of the conservation team pose with Second World War US veteran Huie Lamb (third from right). Behind them is a **P-51 Mustang** which the team lovingly restored to match 'Etta Jeanne' – the aircraft that Lamb flew from Duxford during the war. It is on occasions like these that some of the true rewards of the museum's conservation work can be felt.

IWM_SITE_DUX_001647

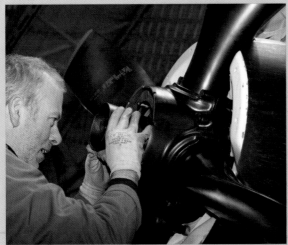

Staff and volunteers (left)

Conservation Officer Andy Marriott refits a propeller to the **P-51 Mustang** as part of preparations to return the plane for display in the **American Air Museum**. The work of the museum staff is complemented by a large team of volunteers (see page 63 for details of how you can get involved).

IWM_SITE_DUX_001647

IN THEIR OWN WORDS – CHRIS KNAPP, CONSERVATION MANAGEMENT

Chris Knapp has worked as part of IWM's conservation team for over a quarter of a century and is now responsible for the museum's large objects, including all the aircraft at Duxford. Here he explains the approach he takes to his job.

My full job title is Head of Large Object Conservation. That basically means that if something's too big to fit on a person's desk it usually lands on mine! And, believe me, the B-52 is a damn big aeroplane to have land on your desk!

My job is about preserving history. If you've got a sponge, it soaks up water. Handle the sponge and the water comes out. Objects soak up history the same way. The more you handle the object the more the history leaks away. That's why our aim at IWM is not only to preserve an object in its original form for as long as possible, but also to do it with minimal intervention.

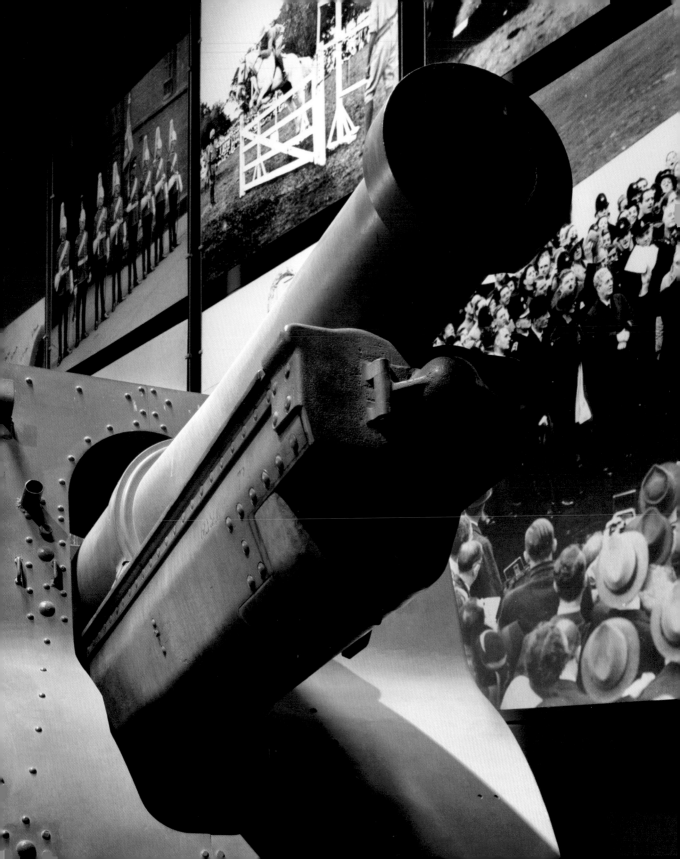

LAND WARFARE

At the far end of the IWM Duxford site, the Land Warfare exhibition features scores of artillery pieces, tanks, trucks and other military vehicles to tell the story of the mechanisation of warfare from the First World War to the present day.

When war broke out in 1914, infantry marched to battle and cavalry rode on horseback – some dressed in their traditional colourful uniforms and equipped with lances and swords. They were met with a hail of fire from machine guns and horse-drawn artillery pieces. Some, like the **German 10.5cm Light Field Howitzer**, were designed to fight side-by-side with the infantry; others operated from a distance to support set-piece battles.

Both sides were forced to dig in along lines that stretched from Switzerland to the Channel coast. More shells and bigger guns were brought in to try to end the deadlock. Motor vehicles like the **American four-wheel drive General Service Truck** came in to use to tow the guns into position. And tanks were invented to break through enemy fortifications and offer protection for advancing infantry.

Such mechanisation did not prove decisive, but by 1918 it had become inextricably linked to the way in which battles were fought. Land warfare would never be the same again.

'We must... avoid long static warfare... and human casualties... Mechanisation... holds out the only hope.'

General Cyril Deverell, Chief of the Imperial General Staff, 1937

53

Proven success (left)
The French 155mm Schneider Heavy Howitzer was designed for use on the Western Front during the First World War. It proved so effective that in the inter-war period many were updated by adding pneumatic tyres.
IWM_SITE_DUX_001567

HITLER'S LIGHTNING STRIKE ON THE ALLIES

In the inter-war period, many traditional military officers advocated a return to pre-1914 methods as a way to put the horror and deadlock of trench warfare behind them. But there were a few forward-thinkers, especially in the German Army, who saw the potential advantages of further mechanisation and developed new tactics to harness them to the full.

The result was 'Blitzkrieg' (Lightning War) — a closely coordinated form of attack carried out by a newly developed all-arms team, the Panzer Division. Aircraft such as the Stuka dive-bomber would operate as 'aerial artillery', blasting enemy defences. Then tanks would smash through at a selected point, quickly followed by mechanised infantry (troops in vehicles rather than on foot) and support arms, such as anti-aircraft guns like the **8.8cm Flak 37 Anti-Aircraft Gun**.

These tactics proved shockingly successful. In May and June 1940 the Germans swept through the Low Countries and France. The British Army was forced to retreat to Dunkirk, from where it was evacuated across the Channel.

DID YOU KNOW?
Before its retreat to Dunkirk, the British Expeditionary Force had to abandon over 60,000 tanks, cars and trucks, and over 20,000 motorcycles — many of which were later used against the Allies by the German Army.

Inferior firepower
The Vickers VI was the principle light tank of the British Army in France in 1940. It proved to be of little use against the carefully coordinated German offensive.
IWM_SITE_DUX_001562

Defensive liability
The 25mm was the standard French Army light anti-tank gun in 1940. It was, however, hopelessly obsolete and more of a nuisance than an effective weapon.
IWM_SITE_DUX_001563

LAND WARFARE TIMELINE
For Britain and the Commonwealth the history of land warfare since 1914 has been shaped by two momentous global conflicts, followed by the threat of nuclear obliteration and subsequent decades of change and uncertainty. It is also a story of vast mechanisation and technological advance.

1914–1918
The First World War is one of entrenched deadlock, vast artillery bombardments and terrible land battles. Aircraft and tanks are used in battle for the first time.

1920s
Britain operates on the assumption that there will not be another war for ten years. Development of the armed forces slows.

IN THEIR OWN WORDS – CAPTAIN HENRY FAURE WALKER

Tactical victim
A knocked-out British Cruiser tank sits by the roadside in France after an engagement on 27 May 1940.
IWM F 4594

'...we had lost the art of using our tanks.'

Henry Faure Walker, a staff officer with the 7th Guards Brigade, was stationed in France when the Germans launched their Blitzkrieg offensive in May 1940. Here he acknowledges that Allied tactics were partly to blame for the eventual outcome.

The Allies had a better and bigger tank force than the Germans but we had lost the art of using our tanks. The French general staff was dominated by infantry-minded generals and although they had many more tanks – and extremely good tanks, every bit as good as the German tanks – instead of keeping them concentrated in armoured divisions and a massive tank force, they broke them up into penny packets and allotted a few tanks to infantry divisions and so they were never effective.

FIGHTBACK IN NORTH AFRICA AND ITALY

By late 1940 the only place that Britain could mount an effective land campaign against the Axis forces was in North Africa. Attacking a large but poorly equipped Italian Army, British forces won a series of victories until the Germans sent reinforcements under the command of General Erwin Rommel.

For the next two years the desert war saw both sides fighting backwards and forwards across the same ground, until the battle of El Alamein in October and November 1942. British victory in this battle, combined with British and American landings in French Morocco and Algeria, forced the Germans to surrender in May 1943. This success owed a great deal to the inspired leadership of British General Bernard Montgomery – often a highly visible

presence close to the front in his **M3A5 General Grant II Medium Tank**.

On Churchill's insistence, the Allies went on to invade Italy in the summer of 1943. Italy surrendered quickly, but the Germans refused to give up their former ally's territory. For much of the rest of the war there would be fierce fighting in the mountainous Italian terrain, with artillery such as the **British 25 Pounder Field Gun** taking over from the tank as the dominant form of attack and defence.

JANUARY 1933
Adolf Hitler rises to power. The German war machine is gradually rebuilt, with the innovative use of mobile armoured 'Panzer' divisions at its centre.

SEPTEMBER 1939
The Second World War begins. The first major land offensive comes in May 1940 when German Panzer divisions smash the Allied defences (right).
IWM RML 318

22 JUNE 1941
Germany invades the Soviet Union with huge initial gains. Later offensives – the last being a vast tank battle at Kursk in 1943 – see German success halted and reversed.

DEFEAT OF THE AXIS FORCES IN EUROPE

When the Nazis invaded the Soviet Union in June 1941, their rapid Blitzkrieg offensive threatened to crush Russian resistance. It was the ultimate use of mechanised warfare – the Germans advanced over 600km (378 miles) in barely three months, only coming to a halt in the face of a harsh Russian winter.

However, over the next two years the Russians showed that they had some very powerful tanks of their own, particularly the **T34/85 Medium Tank**. By 1943, the Red Army had learnt the hard way how to put them to use properly. After the bloody battle at Stalingrad and the largest tank battle ever, at Kursk, the Soviets began to force the Germans to retreat.

On 6 June 1944 – D-Day – the Allies launched their invasion of north-west Europe. The events of D-Day and the subsequent Battle for Normandy are covered by two exhibitions in **Land Warfare**. **The Normandy Experience** looks at the invasion from the point of view of the people who took part

and the equipment they used. And **Monty** tells the story of Field Marshal Viscount Montgomery of Alamein (see right), who drove the Germans and Italians from North Africa, led his 8th Army through Sicily into Italy, and then took command of the ground forces for the invasion and liberation of German-occupied France.

The Normandy Landings caught the Germans off-balance, but they recovered to mount determined opposition. Eventually, though, the Allies began to push their way through France and the Low Countries and on into Germany itself. By 8 May 1945, the war in Europe was over.

Coming ashore (below)
The entrance to The Normandy Experience – via a mocked-up landing craft, used to bring troops to shore – has an audio reconstruction of what it would have been like on D-Day itself.
IWM_SITE_DUX_001680

NOVEMBER 1942	**APRIL-JUNE 1944**	**6 JUNE 1944**	**15 AUGUST 1945**
Britain wins its first major land victory over Germany at El Alamein. Fighting in North Africa, which began in the summer of 1940, continues until May 1943.	The British Army repels a Japanese invasion of India, and slowly begins reversing all the gains made by Japan since it joined the war in 1941.	The Allies land an invasion force in France. By September the German border has been reached. The Allies cross the Rhine in March 1945.	Japan announces that it is surrendering. The war in Europe is already over, ending with the fall of Berlin in May 1945.

EXHIBIT IN FOCUS: MONTY'S CAMPAIGN CARAVANS

Montgomery conducted his campaign in north-west Europe from these three command caravans – one for his office, one for his bedroom and one for his map room.

The caravans were always parked slightly apart from the rest of Tactical Headquarters, which in itself was always separate from, and in advance of, the Main Headquarters of 21st Army Group.

This arrangement afforded 'Monty' the solitude he needed to plan his campaign. And they allowed him to stay close to the front – sometimes only a few miles away from the battle.

Mapping Monty's war (above)
The Map Caravan was the nerve centre of Monty's Tactical Headquarters. Pinned to its walls were maps on which the latest intelligence about operations was plotted.
DUX_2003_040_003

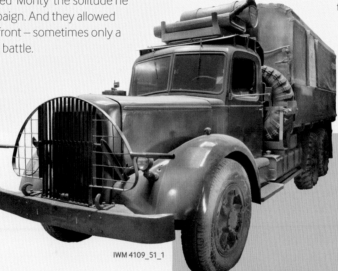

IWM 4109_51_1

Rival claims (below)
Field Marshal Sir Alan Brooke, Winston Churchill and Monty, outside the caravans, June 1944. Churchill and King George VI were the only visitors to whom Monty was prepared to give up the use of his Bedroom Caravan. Captured by the 8th Army from Italian Field Marshal Giovanni Messe in May 1943, it had previously been used by Monty's great adversary Rommel. IWM TR 1838

The Office Caravan contains images of German generals such as Rommel, Model, Kesselring and von Rundstedt. Here Monty explains why:

'I used to look at the photograph of the general I was up against at the moment and try and decide what sort of person he was and how he was likely to react to any moves I might make against him. In some curious way this helped me in the battle.'

'I used to look at the photograph of the general I was up against ...'

THE FORGOTTEN WAR

Japan exploded into the Second World War with a shock attack on the US fleet at Pearl Harbor in 1941. The subsequent war in the Pacific and the Far East took longer to complete than the war in Europe and was fought with gruelling intensity – often in extremes of climate and geography. Fighting in the jungle, for example, placed different requirements on weaponry and equipment. The **British 3.7 in Pack Howitzer**, which could be broken down and carried on mules, proved especially useful in this environment.

Many of the men who fought in the Far East consider themselves to have been part of a 'forgotten army'. To help address this perceived neglect, the lower floor of Land Warfare houses an exhibition called **The Forgotten War**, produced by IWM in partnership with the Burma Star Association.

DID YOU KNOW?

The UK's involvement in Iraq from 2003 to 2011 was codenamed Operation Telic – a little used English word meaning 'purposeful'. Service personnel joked that it stood for 'Tell Everyone Leave is Cancelled'.

BRITAIN IN THE COLD WAR AND BEYOND

After the Second World War, Britain became a founder member of the United Nations (UN) – formed to maintain international peace and security. Then, as the battle lines of the Cold War were drawn, it became a key member of the North Atlantic Treaty Organisation (NATO), designed to face down the threat of the enormous Soviet Army.

Both roles have involved a major military commitment. From 1950 to 1953 British and Commonwealth forces fought in Korea, as part of a UN force against North Korean and Chinese communists. And, from 1945 to 1994, as part of NATO, Britain had to maintain a standing army in Germany – the British Army of the Rhine – investing heavily in tanks like the **Centurion** and **Chieftain**.

Over the same period Britain has also had military commitments closer to home. Until the 1960s its armed forces were regularly employed around the Empire, overseeing the often difficult process of handing over independence – in Palestine, India, Malaya, Kenya, Aden and elsewhere.

Anti-terrorist operations also meant that, at the end of the 1960s, British troops were a fixture on the streets of Northern Ireland. And in 1982, the nation's armed forces successfully liberated the Falkland Islands after the invasion by Argentina.

Britain's wider international commitments have continued in more recent times. In 1991 the British Army fought under the auspices of the UN in the Gulf, and throughout the 1990s British troops were involved in other UN and NATO peacekeeping missions, such as in Bosnia. Then, in the early 2000s, British land forces saw action in Afghanistan and Iraq. The **Saxon Patrol Vehicle** on display in Land Warfare, for example, served in Afghanistan as recently as 2010.

25 AUGUST 1945

The British Army of the Rhine is formed in Germany. As the Cold War ensues, it becomes a key part of the western forces arrayed against the Red Army.

AUGUST 1947

Britain's Indian Empire is divided to create the states of India and Pakistan. Similar transfers of power take place across the Empire in the coming decades.

JUNE 1950

Communist North Korea invades UN-backed South Korea. British troops fight in the war that follows (left), until a ceasefire in July 1953.

IWM MH 33028

Battlefield stalwart
This Soviet T55 Main Battle Tank is one of over 100,000 built between 1958 and 1979. Exported to nearly 40 countries, they have fought in almost every conflict of the past 50 years.

IWM_SITE_DUX_001564

APRIL 1969
British troops are sent to Northern Ireland to stop Protestant attacks on Catholics. They are soon targeted by terrorists in a new form of urban warfare.

APRIL 1982
Argentina invades the Falklands. Britain retakes the islands in June with fighting on land that often involves old-fashioned hand-to-hand combat.

JANUARY 1991
An international coalition goes to war to liberate Kuwait from its Iraqi invaders. The ground war lasts 100 hours and the Iraqis are expelled.

SEPTEMBER 2001
Terrorist attacks on New York and Washington cause Britain to join a US-led invasion of Afghanistan. In 2003 Iraq is also invaded as part of this 'war on terror'.

PARTNER MUSEUMS

As you make your way around IWM Duxford you will come across a number of partner museums, all of which have important stories to tell in their own right. You should also look out for the many war memorials scattered around the site, testament to the airfield's history of wartime service.

The Royal Anglian Regiment Museum
(below left and right)

The Royal Anglian Regiment is one of the most operationally experienced in the British Army today. It was Britain's first 'Large Regiment of Infantry', formed in 1964 from what used to be the ten county regiments of East Anglia and the East Midlands.

Its museum, housed in Land Warfare, uses a series of interactive displays to take you through the regiment's eventful history, and gives you an insight into what life is like for one of its soldiers. For more information, go to royalanglianmuseum.org.uk

IWM_SITE_DUX_001560; IWM_SITE_DUX_001561

> ## 'One of the finest feats of arms in the history of the British Army.'
>
> **Field Marshal Haig on an attack made by the men of the Cambridgeshire Regiment in 1916 on a German stronghold called the Schwaben Redoubt**

The Cambridgeshire Regiment Exhibition (above)

Next to the Royal Anglian Regiment Museum is the Cambridgeshire Regiment Exhibition, which records the regiment's proud hundred-year history before it helped to form the Royal Anglian Regiment in the 1960s.

Manned only by part-time soldiers, the Cambridgeshire Regiment distinguished itself in the Second Anglo-Boer War and both World Wars — winning over 300 awards for gallantry in the First World War alone. IWM_SITE_DUX_001559

Airborne Assault

On 22 June 1940 Winston Churchill ordered the setting up of 'a corps of at least 5,000 parachute troops'. Before the end of the war these airborne forces would serve with distinction in dramatic battles such as the Bruneval Raid, the Normandy landings and the legendary operation to secure the bridge at Arnhem.

So begins the story told in Airborne Assault, the Museum of the Parachute Regiment and Airborne Forces – a story that continues all the way up to the present-day exploits of 16 Air Assault Brigade, the army's rapid response force.

Located within AirSpace, Air Assault uses displays of uniform, weapons, equipment and medals to bring to life the heroism, resourcefulness and professionalism of these brave soldiers who go to war from the air.

IWM_SITE_DUX_000178

MEMORIALS AT IWM DUXFORD

There are many memorials at IWM Duxford. Some are large, others are small. Some relate to entire regiments, others to individuals. All are worth looking out for.

The war memorials at Duxford vary hugely in size and shape. There are sculptures and plinths, books of remembrance and specially planted trees. Perhaps the largest is the 'Wall of Honour' for the Royal Anglian Regiment (right), situated to the right of the path linking the American Air Museum and Land Warfare.

Among the smaller memorials are benches dedicated to individual airmen, all of whom share a link to Duxford. By the south-east corner of **Battle of Britain**, for example, you can find two benches dedicated to Spitfire pilot George 'Grumpy' Unwin (see page 37), who flew from the base during the long summer of 1940.

IWM_SITE_DUX_001558

IWM DUXFORD AND YOU

If you have enjoyed your visit to IWM Duxford, there are several ways to extend that experience – both on the day and on future occasions – and to share it with family, friends or colleagues.

EATING AND DRINKING

The Armoury (below), next to the **Visitor Centre**, offers hot seasonal British food, deli sandwiches, and hot and cold drinks. Children can choose from a selection of lunch bags or hot dishes. The nearby playground makes this a great family choice. Opening hours: daily, 10am-5.30pm (closes 3.30pm during winter trading hours).

The Workshop Restaurant, located between **Air and Sea** and **Battle of Britain**, is an historic building that once housed workshops and stores, such as a carpenter's workshop and a parachute store. The menu includes classics such as the Sally B burger and mac 'n' cheese cooked to order. The Workshop is a fully licensed restaurant selling wine and beer, as well as teas, coffees and soft drinks. Opening hours: daily, 11am-4.30pm (closes 3pm during winter trading hours).

At the **American Air Museum** café you can treat yourself to afternoon tea with a cake or muffin from our freshly baked selection. The café also sells a range of sandwiches, kids lunch bags and hot and cold drinks. Opening hours: daily, 11am-4pm (closes 3pm during winter trading hours).

SHOPPING

The IWM Duxford shop, located in our **Visitor Centre** (right), provides a wide range of inspiring books, DVDs, models, prints, posters, learning resources and a large selection of gifts and souvenirs for all ages. You can also shop online at **iwmshop.org.uk**.

LEARNING

Our Department for Learning offers talks and activities to groups of formal learners from primary schools, secondary schools and colleges, covering subjects related to History, Science, Technology, Engineering and Mathematics.

Teachers are welcome to make free preliminary visits to plan their trip. We are happy to advise on options according to the age of the children, the programme of study and the time available. We also offer online resources to help support any self-directed part of the visit.

For informal learners, we offer daily introductory tours, taster talks and weekend tours. There are also Special Interest Days, pre-booked tours and other regular activities aimed at families and youth groups.

For details, please check **iwm.org.uk/visits/ iwm-duxford/groups**. Alternatively please phone the Public Engagement & Learning team on **01223 499341** or email **dux-edu@iwm.org.uk**.

IWM_SITE_DUX_001619

IWM_SITE_DUX_001627

VOLUNTEERING

There are many volunteering opportunities at IWM Duxford, some administered by IWM and others by the Duxford Aviation Society (DAS). The DAS is the largest and most active group of its kind in Britain, acquiring, preserving and displaying British civil aircraft and military vehicles, and working closely with IWM towards the development of IWM Duxford.

As a volunteer, you could be working on the conservation of aircraft or military vehicles, leading guided tours, or taking on a role in our Visitor Centre. For a list of voluntary roles currently available at IWM Duxford, and for information on joining the DAS, please contact our Volunteer Programme Manager on **01223 499357**.

MEETINGS AND EVENTS

IWM Duxford offers a range of state-of-the-art spaces, facilities and services for events, conferences, meetings, seminars and all forms of corporate hospitality – with close proximity to Cambridge, easy access to the M11 motorway and an unrivalled historic setting.

We have three remarkable indoor spaces suitable for hosting up to 1,000 guests: the breathtaking **AirSpace** exhibition hall, the **Conservation** Hall and the Foster-designed **American Air Museum**. We also offer the purpose-built **AirSpace Conference Centre**, suitable for both small groups and gatherings of up to 200 people.

You can also take advantage of our outdoor spaces, historic buildings, stunning aircraft and remarkable exhibits – entertaining guests at one of our world-famous air shows, hosting your own outdoor event or using the airfield as a backdrop to a photo shoot.

For more information, please contact the Events Team at **iwmduxford@iwmevents.co.uk** or call **01223 497501**.

MEMBERSHIP

For full details of the current membership packages, see **iwm.org.uk/membership**.

ABOUT IWM

IWM is a global authority on conflict and its impact on Britain, its former Empire and Commonwealth, from the First World War to the present day and beyond. We collect objects and stories that give an insight into people's experiences of war, and we preserve them for future generations. By telling these stories on our website – iwm.org.uk – and across our five branches, we aim to help people understand why we go to war and the effect that conflict has on people's lives. As a charity, we rely on admission fees, our cafés, sales in our shops (including iwmshop.org.uk) and donations to continue our work, and to ensure that the stories of those who have lived, fought and died in conflicts since 1914 continue to be heard.

IWM LONDON

In Summer 2014 IWM London re-opened with a transformed new atrium, designed by architects Foster + Partners, as well as ground-breaking new First World War Galleries to mark the 100 year anniversary of the start of the Great War. The 'new' IWM London reveals more of IWM's unique collections, telling important stories of people's experiences of war and conflict up to the present day, including how conflict has divided communities in places such as Ireland, Iraq and Afghanistan.

Lambeth Road, London SE1 6HZ.

IWM NORTH

The multi-award-winning IWM North was designed by world-renowned architect Daniel Libeskind to represent a globe shattered by conflict. The iconic building houses innovative and dynamic exhibitions, including hourly digital media Big Picture Shows designed to explore how war shapes lives. There is also a changing temporary exhibition programme, as well as regular public events all aimed at inspiring knowledge and encouraging debate.

The Quays, Trafford Wharf Road, Manchester M17 1TZ.

CHURCHILL WAR ROOMS

Inside Churchill War Rooms lie the original Cabinet War Rooms – the secret underground bunker which sheltered Churchill and his staff during the Second World War. Explore the historic rooms, including the Map Room where the books and charts are exactly where they were left when the door was locked in 1945. Discover the stories of those who worked underground as London was bombed above them, and explore the life and legacy of Winston Churchill in the Churchill Museum.

Clive Steps, King Charles Street, London SW1A 2AQ.

HMS BELFAST

HMS *Belfast* is the most significant surviving Second World War Royal Navy warship, with a history that extends to the Cold War, Korea and beyond. Once home to a crew of up to 950 men, HMS *Belfast* tells the stories of those who lived on board this warship. Explore nine decks of seafaring history including the machines in the Engine Room that powered her across the world. Hear the sailors' battle stories and take control of a fleet in the Operations Room.

The Queen's Walk, London SE1 2JH.

For information relating to all IWM branches, please call 020 7416 5000 or go to the website: iwm.org.uk